HEAVYWEIGHT BOXING CHAMPIONS

BOXING FROM THE BEGINNING

TERRY MIDDLETON

authorHOUSE®

AuthorHouse™
1663 Liberty Drive
Bloomington, IN 47403
www.authorhouse.com
Phone: 833-262-8899

Published by AuthorHouse 05/25/2021

ISBN: 978-1-6655-2200-7 (sc)
ISBN: 978-1-6655-2203-8 (e)

Library of Congress Control Number: 2021907236

Print information available on the last page.

"Boxing is the sport and art of punching your opponent inside the ring without getting punched in return."

CONTENTS

Foreword xi

History Of Boxing 1

Governing Bodies Of Boxing 3

The 44 Bare Knuckle Champions (1719-1892) 12

Gloved Heavyweight Boxing Champions.................21

John L. (Lawrence) Sullivan................................ 26

"Gentleman Jim" Corbett 29

Bob Fitzsimmons 32

James J. (Jackson) Jeffries 35

Marvin Hart.. 38

Tommy Burns...41

Jack Johnson... 44

Jess Willard 47

Jack Dempsey 50

Gene Tunney 54

Max Schmeling 57

Jack Sharkey 65

Primo Carnera 70

Max Baer 76

James J. Braddock 82

Joe Louis 88

Ezzard Mack Charles 95

Jersey Joe Walcott 100

Rocky Maricano 105

Floyd Patterson 115

Ingemar Johansson.. 123

Charles "Sonny" Liston 128

Muhammad Ali.. 136

Jimmy Ellis 149

Joe Frazier 155

George Foreman 162

Leon Spinks 170

Kenny Norton... 175

Larry Holmes 180

Michael Spinks.. 186

Mike Tyson... 192

James Douglas 201

Evander Holyfield 206

Riddick Bowe 213

Michael Moorer... 219

Shannon Briggs... 224

Lennox Lewis.. 228

Hasim Rahman.. 235

Wladimir Klitschko 241

Tyson Fury 248

Anthony Joshua 254

Andy Ruiz Jr..259

Heavyweight Boxing Quiz 263

Kentuckiana Boxing Trainers 270

Author's Note 277

FOREWORD

This book is dedicated to my grandfather, Clarence Middleton, who boxed while in the United States Army during WWI, and my father, Dennis Middleton who boxed while in the United States Navy during WWII.

My first memories were watching my Dad workout when I was a little kid. He used Boxing and weight training to exercise after the war.

I picked up on Boxing myself when I was in high school in 1963 and started other Martial Arts in 1968. I found that regular training was a challenging and exciting way to learn different Arts while maintaining physical fitness.

I wanted to respectfully condense and summarize the lives of the Bare Knuckle and Gloved World Heavy Weight Boxing Champions, so a person could meet these men, take a mini-view of their lives, and learn the highlights of their career.

These Boxing pioneers paved the way for athletes to safely box competitively while the average person could box as a physical fitness routine which is exciting, motivating, and get the benefit of self-defense. My gym has had many competitors and Champions, but also have countless students that don't compete and only want the many benefits that only Boxing offers.

It would only be proper to give respect to other weight classes and mention the early "Bare Knuckle"

Fighters. This includes "rough and tumble" men such as Tom Sharkey, Jem Mace, Paddy Ryan, Charles Mitchell, Jake Kiltrain and the first American "Bare Knuckle" Champion, Tom Hyer in 1849.

These amazing men fought in an almost "Anything Goes" brawls that sometimes lasted more than 100 rounds. They fought without gloves, sometimes in the blistering sun, on dirt floors of barns, race tracks, and riverboats.

Many cities or states did not permit these "fist fights" to take place. If the authorities caught the contestants fighting, they could be arrested. Even if the bouts were authorized, the police could stop a bout when they decided it was in the best interest of all concerned.

HISTORY OF BOXING

F ighting with the fists dates back to the beginning of time. Actually, Boxing can be traced back to the Sumerians, five thousand years ago, but became more organized with the Greeks. They incorporated Boxing into the Olympic Games in 688 BC, and it became one of their favorite sports. The rules were few with no weight classes or time limits. Their Roman neighbors quickly added the sport of Boxing to their world and developed their own style which was displayed in the famous "Arena."

Modern-day Boxing was born in the British Iles, a former Roman colony. In 1719, James Figg, a master fencer, opened the first Boxing school in London, England. Figg defeated all opponents and is recognized as the first organized Boxing champion, and deemed the "Father of Modern Boxing."

Boxing rules before 1743 were very few, as much mayhem was displayed in the ring. Jack Broughton, a James Figg student, and future Champion became a highly skilled and ferocious Boxer. On April 24, 1741, Broughton met George Stevenson for a Championship Bare-Knuckle bout in London, England. Broughton beat Stevenson so severely that he died a few days later. Broughton was so distraught, that he set out to make Boxing safer for the contestants. He introduced a new set of rules simply called the "Broughton's Rules" that took effect August 16, 1743. He reinvented a softer boxing glove, added more rules, and promoted the skills and science of Boxing, which limited the brutality of the sport. In 1838, the rules slightly changed and were called "The London Prize Ring Rules", but changed again in 1866 to the present basic rules. The English Boxing Association passed this latest set of rules devised by John Sholto Douglas, the "Marquess of Queensberry" in Scotland. Douglas, a lightweight Boxing Champion himself, wanted to make the sport of Boxing even safer. His much safer and fairer rules came to be known as the "Marquess of Queensberry" Rules. The use of these rules began in 1889 in the US during the reign of John L. Sullivan.

GOVERNING BODIES
OF BOXING

The Olympics Committee is an International organization that holds competitions for many sports every four years that includes Boxing. The ancient Olympic Games began in 688BC in the European country of Greece. Incidentally, Onomastos from the city of Smyrna, a Greek colony, was the winner of the first gold medal in Boxing.

Modern Olympic Games resumed in 1896, later Boxing was included in 1904 Games in St. Louis, Missouri. All "pagan activities" were halted in AD 393 by Christian Emperor Theodosius I. Since 1904, America has nearly doubled all other countries in Gold, Silver, and Bronze medals!

The AAU, Amateur Athletic Union was founded by James L. Sullivan on January 21, 1888 to develop common standards and rules in participation and competition. This American organization governs all amateur sports including Boxing. One of the major goals of this union is to enhance America's chances in the Olympic Games. However, many competitors have gotten tremendous benefits from this organization of sports.

Most Boxers develop their skills through an amateur program before entering the professional ranks. Modern amateur Boxing has also been an

Olympic sport since 1904. To maintain fairness and safety, there are weight divisions from Flyweight through Super Heavyweight. The spread is generally about seven pounds or so.

The AIBA, Amateur International Boxing Association was founded in 1946 to organize and govern many State Boxing organizations from around the world.

The IBU, International Boxing Union was the first professional governing body that was founded in June 1911 in Paris, France. It was active until Nazi Germany took over the group during WWII. They renamed the affiliation The Associazione Pugilistica Professionistica Europea, APPE. After the war, the original group briefly reunited only to dissolve the old group and form the new European Boxing Union, EBU, in 1946. A modern, and completely different IBU was founded in Atlanta, Georgia in 1996. The current EBU is not one of the big four major governing bodies.

Presently in the US, several states have Professional Boxing Commissions, with Commissioners who enforce state rules and regulations. The rules are to keep the sport of Boxing safe, fair and honest.

There are several professional World Boxing Associations that promote the sport. The World Boxing Association (WBA), the World Boxing Council (WBC), the World Boxing Organization (WBO), the International Boxing Federation (IBF), and a few smaller organizations. Each organization ranks their Boxers and has their Champion prizefighter in each weight division. Many times, a world contender or Champion is not ranked the same by every organization. When one Champion has an opportunity to meet and beat the Champion of all major organizations, he is considered the "Undisputed Champion of the World." All Champions must defend their title within a specified period of time, or they must relinquish their title. The term "lineal" means that the title has been consistently won from all previous Champions.

These professional organizations control and govern the world of Boxing. These governing bodies were founded to develop rules, maintain fairness and honesty, sanction matches, oversee negotiations, and determine rankings including the lineal Champions. The groups can recognize each other's rules, regulations, and rankings when appropriate and desired. These associations can also negotiate technicalities for certain contests or championship bouts.

The WBA, World Boxing Association is the most prestigious of the big four professional, major governing bodies today. It began in 1921 as The National Boxing Association in the US by thirteen state representatives. The name was changed to WBA in 1962 as a world organization and the headquarters are in Panama City, Panama. The first bout under this jurisdiction was Jack Dempsey and Georges Carpentier that was held on July 2, 1921 in Jersey City, New Jersey.

The WBC, World Boxing Council is the second most prestigious group and was founded in 1963. In 1983, this body was the first to shorten championship bouts to 12 rounds from 15 for the safety of the contestants. Today, it has 161 member countries participating and the headquarters are in Mexico City, Mexico.

The IBF, The International Boxing Federation is located in Springfield, New Jersey. This group was devised after New Jersey Commissioner, Bobby Lee Sr. was unhappy after not being chosen as the president of the WBA in an annual convention in Puerto Rico. The original name of this body was United States Boxing Association- International, but the name was changed to IBF in 1984.

The WBO, The World Boxing Organization has its headquarters in San Juan, Puerto Rico. Businessmen from Puerto Rico and the Dominican Republic formed this organization in 1988 after a dispute over rules and regulations with the WBA in an annual convention in Venezuela. This group was not highly recognized for nearly twenty years, but is now acknowledged alongside the WBA, WBC, and the IBF.

The Ring Magazine was founded by Nat Fleischer in 1922 in Blue Bell, Pennsylvania and became known as "The Bible of Boxing". This magazine published articles of Wrestling and Boxing and recognized its own contenders and champions. Champion, Oscar de la Hoya acquired this failing institution in 2007 and moved its headquarters to Los Angeles, California.

The WBHOF, World Boxing Hall of Fame was the first organization to recognize the elite Champions of Boxing. This affiliation was founded in Riverside,

California in 1980, but never had a permanent location or museum. Ten years later another organization emerged and is now more recognized for its selections called the IBHOF.

The IBHOF, The International Boxing Hall of Fame was founded in 1990 and recognizes the big four professional governing body Champions. The Champions who are inducted into the Hall of Fame are recognized for their outstanding achievements. This association is based in Canastota, California.

Organized fighting was the product of the occupation in the days of the Roman Empire. During the 1600's, "Prize Fighting" became very popular in Great Britain. "Rough and tumble" challengers and Champions would travel the countryside stopping in the towns and villages to attract eager crowds to watch two men fight. They did so to gain fame and fortune through fighting. These men would seek challenges from the villagers, but if they had no takers, they would perform exhibitions. Either way, these visits would generate revenue for themselves. Many times, these Pugilists had backers that put up betting monies for them to compete against all challengers. The term for this prize money became known as the "purse."

When the crowd did assemble, they were instructed to form a circle. The men in the front row would hold a rope to give the contestants room to compete. This area became known as the "ring." If there was a "local" that wanted to try his luck against these traveling Pugilists, he would "throw his hat into the ring." This phrase is still used today for various attempts. If no one took up the challenge, the travelers would begin an exhibition for the crowd. The spectators would cheerfully throw money into the ring to show their appreciation.

As the popularity grew for these events, a need for a better fighting area was needed for the fighters and spectators. So, promoters drove wooden stakes into the ground with four corners and a rope or ropes were strung to each stake that made a square competition zone. However, the term "ring" continued to be used then and even today. Prize money or the "purse" was nailed to one of the stakes for everyone to see. This is where the term "Stakes" for betting originated.

In 1790, a Boxer named Daniel Mendoza designed an area that had a gate installed in order to charge spectators to witness his bout. The term "Gate" originated here to define fees paid at the door for productions of any kind.

In those days, as today, the objective of a Boxing match was to win by beating your opponent until he gave up or was knocked out. The rules then were few and about just anything was fair. The match went as many rounds as needed to have a winner and a round lasted until one man was knocked down. After a knockdown, there was a 30 second rest period for both contestants. If one fighter could not come back to a starting line scratched on the floor, he was counted out after 8 seconds. This was the origination of the phrase "Counted Out." Additionally, "Toe the Line" phrase began from the rule to return to the scratched line on the floor after the rest period ended.

A contestant could have two helpers that became known as "Seconds." They could help the fighter when needed in the rest periods or box a secondary bout if required.

In 1824 the first grandstand arena was constructed for Boxing events which collapsed twice killing one and injuring several.

Prizefighting became very popular and entertaining to the average person, sophisticates, and even aristocrats in England. However, since there was much mayhem inside and out the ring, the local law enforcement officials were not so enthusiastic. This caused some counties in England to ban "Prizefighting". However, the promoters would hold the matches anyway and used clever disguises and deceptions to carry on. For example, a promoter would stage a bout near the county line. If the Sheriff showed up to arrest the principals, a short step across the county line could avoid apprehension.

Many great Irish and English Boxers came to America in the late 1700's and 1800's because much of England outlawed prizefighting. Here in the US, some of these men held Boxing events much like in their homeland. In addition, Irish and English sailors plus other immigrants came to America to scrap near the bars in the ports to make side money and develop a fighting career.

The first US prize fight under the "London Prize

Ring Rules" was in 1816 in New York by an audience. It was between Jacob Hyer and Tom Beasley. Hyer won and self-proclaimed himself to be the first American champion. However, most believe his son, Tom Hyer was actually the first American Champion by beating George McChester in New York in 1841 in a grueling 101 rounds. In the very next year, in 1842, Irish-American, Tom McCoy fought Englishmen Chris Lilly in a 120-round match. McCoy died as a result, which caused the U.S. government to make prizefighting illegal in the country.

Englishman, Paddy Ryan became a US resident and beat Englishman Joe Goss and also claimed to be the first American World Champion in 1880 at Colliers Station, West Virginia.

Weight Divisions

Divisions	Weights
Heavyweight	200+ lbs
Light heavyweight	168–175 lbs
Middleweight	154–160 lbs
Welterweight	140–147 lbs
Lightweight	130–135 lbs
Featherweight	122–126 lbs
Bantamweight	115–118 lbs
Flyweight	108–112 lbs

THE 44 BARE KNUCKLE CHAMPIONS (1719-1892)

James Figg - Englishman, who was a swordsman that owned a fencing school in London, England. He opened the first Boxing school and amphitheater to train students and host bouts. He also built an elevated stage with an area of containing rails to feature these bouts and exhibitions. Figg is also considered the first Boxing Champion and the "Father of Modern Boxing." Champion: 1719-1730.

Jack Broughton - Englishman who beat George Taylor, a Figg student. Taylor felt that he should automatically claim the title when James Figg died in 1740. Broughton opened his own operation and proposed safer rules than was being used. He proposed the new rules after his bout with George Stevenson who died following their bout in 1741. The "Jack Broughton" rules were adopted in 1743 that designed padded gloves for sparring and barred excessive fouls. However, the rules left wrestling, and throwing type moves legal. Broughton was more of a Boxer than brawler. Champion: 1734-1750.

Jack Slack - Englishman was the grandson of James Figg. Jack faced Champion Jack Broughton and struggled until he managed to land a lucky punch that closed both eyes of Broughton. It's said that Slack was a dirty fighter and a shady character. Champion: 1750-1760.

Bill Stevens – Englishman, who was an excellent Boxer with a dominant right hand and could take great punishment. He beat Jack Broughton on June 11, 1760. Champion: 1760-1761.

George Meggs - Englishman who was regarded as slow, clumsy, and not very talented. However, he beat Bill Stevens. It's said that he would throw a fight. Champion: 1761-1762.

George Millson - Englishman who was strong and tough, but was not a very talented Boxer. He did enough to beat George Meggs and reigned for six years. Champion: 1765-1771.

Tom Juchau - Englishman who fought the best Boxers of his time and beat Champion George Millson. Champion: 1771-1776.

Peter Corcoran - Irishman who was a skillful, hard hitter that beat William Darts in just one minute. He was the first Irishman to win the title. He rose to the top in the Boxing world but died in poverty. Champion: 1771-1776.

William Darts - Englishman who was tricky and skillful, but not very ambitious. He supposedly lost to Peter Corcoran in just one minute in 1776. Champion 1766-1769.

Tom Lyons - Englishman who had a strong, tough street fighting style who became Champion. Champion: 1769-1776

Harry Sellers - Englishman was a Jack Slack student. He beat Peter Corcoran in 1776 in a questionable match. Champion 1776-1779.

Jack Fearns - Irishman who was the second to hold the title from his country. Champion: 1779-1783

Tom Johnson - Englishman who wildly missed once with a punch and hit the corner post and broke his hand during a bout. However, he eventually became Champion, was inducted into "The Ring" Hall of Fame, and the International Boxing Hall of Fame in 1995. Champion 1783-1791.

Benjamin Brain - Englishman who was a very good Boxer that won in just two rounds over Tom Johnson on January 17, 1791, and died the Champion in 1794. Champion: 1791-1794.

Daniel Mendoza - Englishman of Spanish and Jewish descent. He is the first Jewish Champion and was a very strategic and scientific Boxer. He was first to build a perimeter wall with a gate for spectators to pay to enter and watch the bouts. The term "Gate" originated from this action to represent the income earned from paying spectators. Daniel later traveled to Ireland to teach the art of Boxing throughout the country. He is credited with large origins of Boxing there. Champion: 1794-1795.

John Jackson - Englishman who took the title from Daniel Mendoza by holding his hair and repeatedly punching him in the face in an eleven-minute bout. Jackson also started his own Boxing school in London, England. Champion: 1795-1796.

Tom Owen - Englishman who beat William Hooper in 50 rounds. He is credited with inventing the "Dumbbell." Champion: 1796-1797.

Jack Bartholomew - Englishman who was fast, powerful, and a good Boxer that beat Tom Owen in just 30 minutes. Champion: 1797-1800.

Jem Belcher - Englishman who was the grandson of Jack Slack. He was a very agile and quick Boxer. He is credited with putting colors on the corner posts of the ring. Champion: 1800-1805.

Henry Pearce - Englishman who was Champion and retired due to ill health. Champion: 1805-1807.

John Gully - Englishman who once landed in debtor prison. However, after his release, he became Champion, successful, wealthy, and a member of Parliament. Champion: 1807-1808.

Tom Cribb - Englishman who became Champion and a national hero. In retirement, he became a Boxing trainer. Champion: 1808-1822.

Tom Spring – Englishman, who was a student of Tom Cribb. Cribb retired as Champion and named Spring as his successor. Spring met Jack Langan to confirm his title in 77 rounds. The first grandstand for a Boxing event was constructed. Champion: 1823-1824.

Tom Cannon - Englishman who won the title, retired, became poor, and committed suicide. Champion:1824-1825.

Jem Ward - Englishman who is said to have been a shady character and was accused of betting on himself to lose intentionally. He was the first Champion to be awarded a Championship Title Belt. This was the beginning of today's recognition award for the Champion. Champion: 1825-1832.

Peter Crawley - Englishman who beat Jem Ward on January 2, 1827, in the 11th round. He retired two days later, the shortest reign in Boxing history. Jem Ward self-reclaimed the title and fought challenger Simon Byrne to officially regain the championship. Champion: 1827-1827.

Samuel O'Rourke - Irishman Champion who claimed to have never been beaten. He came to America and started a Boxing school. He also lived in Canada for some time. Champion: 1833-1837.

James Burke - Englishman who claimed the title when Jem Ward retired. Harry Malone challenged Burke and lost. Simon Byrne challenged and lost in a three hour and forty-five-minute bout and died as a result. This promoted the change to safer, "London Prize Ring Rules" of 1838. Champion: 1833-1839.

William Thompson - Englishman who was a smaller than average, but beat bigger opponents including James Burke to become the Champion. Champion: 1839-1850.

Tom Hyer - American who was the son of Boxer, Jacob Hyer who beat George McChester in New York in 1841 after 101 rounds. Tom was considered the first true American Champion. Champion: 1841-1851.

William Perry - Englishman who became Champion after William Thompson retired with a win over Tom Paddock. Champion: 1850-1851.

Harry Broome - Englishman who became Champion with a win over William Perry by a foul on September 29, 1851. Champion: 1851-1859.

John Morrisey - American who faced James Ambrose in 1853. Morrisey was losing the bout until his mobster friends caused chaos which led Morrisey to be declared the Champion. Champion: 1853- 1859.

Tom Paddock - Englishman who beat Harry Broome in 51 rounds on May 19, 1856. Champion: 1856-1858.

Tom Sayers - Englishman who was only 5'8" and 150 pounds that beat Tom Paddock on June 16, 1858, in one hour and twenty minutes, which was 21 rounds. Sayers died at 39 years old and thousands of people attended his funeral. Champion: 1858-1860.

Tom King - Englishman who was a very talented Boxer that beat John Heenan in 1863. He retired, married into wealth, and became very successful. Champion: 1863-1863.

Joe Coburn - Irish/American who was a very "rough and rowdy" man that beat John Heenan in 1863. Champion: 1863-1865.

Jem Mace - Englishman who came to America, fought, and beat Tom Allen in Louisiana in 1870 in just ten rounds. Mace began travelling to many other countries and taught the art of Boxing while holding Boxing tournaments. Champion: 1866-1871.

Mike McCoole - American who claimed the title after Tom Sayers retired. McCoole defended his claim in May 1863 in Charleston, Maryland, but lost to Joe Coburn in 1869. Champion: 1863-1869.

Tom Allen -Englishman who defeated Mike McCoole in St. Louis in 1869. McCoole claimed the title that Joe Coburn left open. McCoole won by a questionable foul after being outclassed. Champion: 1873-1876.

Joe Goss - Englishman who lost to Jem Mace three times, so in Mace's absence, Goss squared off against Tom Allen in Covington, Kentucky in 1876. Goss won by a questionable disqualification after being pounded by Allen. Champion: 1876-1880.

Larry Foley - Australian who was an undefeated Champion. He began his career in a street gang in Sydney, Australia. Champion: 1879-1883.

Paddy Ryan - Irish/American who challenged Joe Goss in West Virginia in 1880 and won in 86 rounds. Ryan also claimed to be the first American Champion. Champion: 1880-1882.

John L. Sullivan - American of Irish descent who beat Paddy Ryan in February 1882 in just ten minutes in Mississippi City, Mississippi. Sullivan had colossal bouts with others like Charley Mitchell and Jake Kiltrain. John L. Sullivan is the last Bare-Knuckle Champion, but he defended his crown wearing gloves as well. Therefore, many consider him as the first gloved Champion as well. Champion: 1882-1892.

GLOVED HEAVYWEIGHT BOXING CHAMPIONS

JOHN L. SULLIVAN　　　　Boston, MA

February 7, 1882 - September 7, 1892

JIM CORBETT　　　　San Francisco, CA

September 7, 1892 - March 17, 1897

BOB FITZSIMMONS　　　　Cornwall, England

March 17, 1897 - June 9, 1899

JAMES J. JEFFRIES　　　　Carroll, OH

June 9, 1899 - September 3, 1905

MARVIN HART　　　　Louisville, KY

September 3, 1905 - February 23, 1906

TOMMY BURNS　　　　Hanover, Ontario

February 23, 1906 - December 26, 1908

JACK JOHNSON　　　　Galveston, TX

December 26, 1908 - April 5, 1915

JES WILLARD　　　　Pottawatomie, KS

April 5, 1915 - July 4, 1919

JACK DEMPSEY　　　　Manassa, CO

July 4, 1919 - September 23, 1926

GENE TUNNEY   New York, NY

September 23, 1926 - January 7, 1931

MAX SCHMELING   Kleinluckow, Prussia

June 12, 1930 - June 21, 1932

JACK SHARKEY   Binghamton, New York

June 21, 1932 - June 29, 1933

PRIMO CARNERA   Sequals, Italy

June 29, 1933 - June 14, 1934

MAX BAER   Omaha, Nebraska

June 14, 1934 - June 13, 1935

JAMES J. BRADDOCK   New York City, New York

June 13, 1935 - June 22, 1937

JOE LOUIS   Lafayette, Alabama

June 22, 1937 - March 1, 1949

EZZARD MACK CHARLES   Lawrenceville, Georgia

September 27, 1950 - July 18, 1951

JERSEY JOE WALCOTT   Pennsauken, New jersey

July 18, 1951 - September 23, 1952

ROCKY MARICANO   Brockton Massachusetts

September 23, 1952 - April 27,1956

HEAVYWEIGHT BOXING CHAMPIONS

FLOYD PATTERSON   Waco, North Carolina

November 30, 1956 - June 26, 1959

June 20, 1960 – September 25, 1962

INGEMAR JOHANSSON   Gothernburg, Sweden

June 26, 1959 - June 20, 1960

CHARLES "SONNY" LISTON   San Slough, Arkansas

September 25, 1962 - February 25, 1964

MUHAMMAD ALI   Louisville, KY

February 25, 1964 - Ret. 1967

January 28, 1974- February 1, 1978

August 15, 1978 - Ret. 1979

JIMMY ELLIS   Louisville, KY

April 27, 1968 - February 16, 1970

JOE FRAZIER   Beaufort, SC

February 16, 1970 - January 22, 1973

GEORGE FOREMAN   Marshall, TX

January 22, 1973- October 5, 1974

November 5, 1994 - November 22, 1997

LEON SPINKS   St. Louis, MO

February 15, 1978 - September 15, 1978

KENNY NORTON   Jacksonville, IL

March 3, 1973 - September 10, 1973

March 18, 1978 - June 9, 1978

LARRY HOLMES   Easton, PA

June 9, 1980 - May 20, 1985

MICHAEL SPINKS   St. Louis, MO

Lt. Heavy March 18, 1983 - September 21, 1985

Heavyweight September 21, 1985 - June 27, 1988

MIKE TYSON   Brooklyn, NY

November 22, 1986 - February 11, 1990

March 16, 1996 - November 9, 1996

BUSTER DOUGLAS   Columbus, OH

February 1, 1990 - October 25, 1990

EVANDER HOLYFIELD   Atmore, AL

October 25, 1990 - November 13, 1992

November 6, 1993 - November 4, 1995

November 9. 1996 - November 13, 1999

August 12, 2000 - March 3, 2001

RIDDICK BOWE   Brooklyn, New York

Nov. 13, 1992 to Nov. 6,1993

MICHAEL MOORER   Brooklyn, New York

Apr. 22, 1994 to Nov. 5, 1994

HEAVYWEIGHT BOXING CHAMPIONS

SHANNON BRIGGS   Brooklyn, New York

Nov. 22,1997 to Mar. 28, 1998

LENNOX LEWIS   London, England

Mar. 28, 1998 to Apr. 22, 2001

Nov. 17, 2001 to Retirement

HASIM RAHMAN   Baltimore, Maryland

Apr. 22, 2001 to Nov. 17, 2001

WLADIMIR KLITSCHKO   Semey, Kazakhstan

Jun. 20, 2009 to Nov. 28, 2015

TYSON FURY   Manchester, England

Nov. 28, 2015 to Oct. 12, 2016

To present lineal Champion

ANTHONY JOSHUA   Hertfordshire, England

Apr. 29, 2017 to Jun.1, 2019

December 7, 2019 to Present

ANDY RUIZ JR.   Imperial, California

June 1, 2019 to December 7, 2019

JOHN L.
(LAWRENCE) SULLIVAN

"Boston Strong Boy"

**B. October 15, 1858 – D. February
2, 1918 Born: Boston MA
5' 10"/ 212.8 lbs.
Record: 40-1-2 34 KO's (1 NC)**

Champion:

February 7, 1882 - September 7, 1892

I rish/American John L. Sullivan was the "larger than life" last "Bare-Knuckle Champion" and first Heavyweight Champion to compete wearing boxing gloves. As a child, young John was a good student who also attended Boston College, but in 1875, he became bored and dropped out to play professional baseball. He soon drifted away from the baseball field and gravitated toward the sport of Boxing. His new career ultimately led him to the "Bare-Knuckle" Championship.

John L. knocked out Champion Paddy Ryan in February of 1882 in Mississippi City, MS to win the "Bare-Knuckle" Championship under the "London Prize Ring Rules." In 1883 and 1884, John L. and fellow boxers traveled the country doing exhibition bouts and public challenges. He offered to fight anyone for money and eventually participated in 450 matches. After about six years, John L. signed on to fight expert Boxer Jake Kiltrain, in Hattiesburg, Mississippi for the very last Bare-Knuckle Championship under the "London Prize Ring Rules." Sullivan was knocked down in the 44th round, but rose to win in the 75th round after Kiltrain's manager threw in the towel.

John L. was the last Bare-Knuckle Champion, but defended his title with and without gloves during his reign as Champion. He would gladly fight with whatever the agreement called for. However, he seemed to prefer wearing boxing gloves, which naturally protects the skin, bones of the hands, and the opponent's face. During John L.'s reign, the rules were changed to the new "Marquess of Queensbury" rules that began in the US in 1889. These rules required Boxers to wear padded gloves, and it also eliminated throwing opponents around much like wrestling. Therefore, most experts would call John L. Sullivan the last Bare-Knuckle Champion and the first Gloved Champion.

Three years later, Boxing fans were shocked and dismayed when John L. was knocked out by the younger and bigger "Gentleman Jim" Corbett in the 21st round on September 7, 1892, in New Orleans, Louisiana. However, Sullivan came to this Championship bout after several years of hard living and little preparation for the match.

After losing the title, John L. had a few more bouts, and several exhibitions matches. He also stayed busy as an actor, speaker, celebrity sports umpire, sports reporter, and bar owner. John L. was inducted into the original International Boxing Hall of Fame in 1990. The dual Heavyweight Champion earned a million dollars in his career, but had only ten dollars in his pocket when he died on February 2, 1918, at age 59 of a heart attack. He was buried in Mount Calvary Cemetery, Roslindale, Massachusetts. John L. Sullivan is still one of the most famous Boxers of all time!

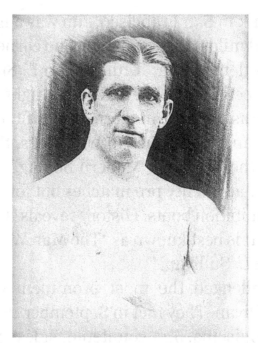

"GENTLEMAN JIM" CORBETT

B. Sept. 1, 1866 – D. Feb. 18, 1933
Born: San Francisco, CA
6' 1" / 185 lbs.
Record: 11-4-3 5 KO's (2 NC)

Champion:
September 7, 1892 - March 2, 1897

Like John L. Sullivan, "Gentleman Jim" Corbett was an Irish/American, but from the west coast of America. Jim came from a middle-class family, attended college, and became a bank clerk at the

Nevada Bank in San Francisco. Jim was a handsome, refined, and mild-mannered man who earned his ring name, "Gentleman Jim." Unlike John L. Sullivan, he wasn't a street fighter, but learned to fight in Boxing gyms. He was the first modern, scientific Boxer who used skills and techniques to win bouts. Some have called him the "Father of Modern Boxing."

He only had twenty pro matches but fought in well over 150 exhibition bouts. History reveals "Gentleman Jim" Corbett is best known as "The Man Who Beat the Great John L. Sullivan"!

Jim challenged the most prominent Champion John L. Sullivan. They met in September 1892 in New Orleans, Louisiana. Jim countered, sidestepped, and pounded the Champion until a right cross knocked out the Champ in the 21st round to make "Gentleman" Jim Corbett the new Boxing King.

Jim reigned until challenged by Bob Fitzsimmons in March 1897 in Carson City, Nevada. Fitzsimmons ended Jim's reign by knocking him out in the 14th round.

Fitzsimmons lost to James J. Jeffries in 1899 and gave Jim another title shot in 1900. Jeffries was too much for Gentleman Jim, and knocked him out in the 23rd round. Former Champion Jim challenged Jefferies to a rematch in 1903 but lost this time in the 10th round. Shortly after this fight, Gentleman Jim retired from the ring.

Jim was also an actor during his Championship reign and continued well into retirement. He was in more than twelve Broadway plays, movies, and was also portrayed in the film "The Roar of the Crowd," by actor Errol Flynn.

"Gentleman Jim" Corbett was the second gloved Heavyweight Champion of the World and was inducted into the International Boxing Hall of Fame in 1990. "The Ring" magazine inducted him into their Hall of Fame in 1954.

"Gentleman Jim" Corbett died on February 18, 1933, at the age of 66 from heart disease and was buried in Cypress Abby Mausoleum, Brooklyn, New York.

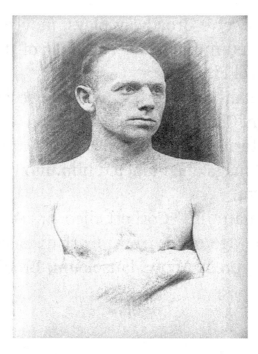

BOB FITZSIMMONS

B. May 26, 1863 – D. October 22, 1917
Born: Helston, Cornwall England
5' 11" / 160 lbs.
Record: 59-8-4 48 KO's

Champion:
March 17, 1897 - June 9, 1899

British, Bob Fitzsimmons was one of twelve Irish/ English siblings who lived in several countries before settling in America. His family left England for New Zealand in 1873 where he picked up several odd jobs before becoming a blacksmith at his brother's business. This physically demanding job is believed to have contributed to his extraordinary strength.

In the 1880s, Jem Mace, an English Bare-Knuckle Boxer, visited and hosted New Zealand's first Boxing tournament. Bob entered the contest and scored several knockouts to win the tourney. Fitz moved on to Australia in the 1880s and turned pro in 1883 with 28 pro fights. To pursue a more significant career, Bob moved once more to America. In 1891 he won his first world title in New Orleans in a thirteen-round middleweight beat down of Jack Dempsey, (not the Heavyweight Champion Jack Dempsey). Fitz added three more wins and one draw.

Even though Bob was a middleweight, he challenged the Heavyweight Champion "Gentleman Jim" Corbett in 1897. Bob, the Middleweight Champion, hit Corbett with punches at will before knocking him out in the 14th round with his famed solar plexus punch to become the third gloved World Heavyweight Champion.

In 1893, Bob took part in a slugfest knocking out seven men in one night in fewer than nineteen rounds, and one of the men being a giant at 6' 7" and 240 pounds. Fitzsimmons' reign lasted two years until James J. Jefferies took the title in June 1899. Jefferies won in the eleventh round by overpowering Fitz with his size at Coney Island, NY. However, Bob continued his career on the road and agreed to a rematch with Jefferies in San Francisco, CA in 1902. In this rematch, Bob caused much damage, but the 50 pounds heavier, and much younger Jefferies eventually knocked out the ex-Champ in the 8th round. A third title shot bout was offered in 1903, but was another defeat as Fitzsimmons' manager stopped the fight in the 10th round.

In 1903, Bob dropped down to compete and win the World Light Heavyweight Championship in 20 rounds to become the first Champion to win titles in three different weight divisions. Fitzsimmons is considered by many, as one of the hardest punchers of all time.

Bob also made a substantial amount of money in his career, but died broke on October 23, 1917, at age 54 of pneumonia. Sadly, there is only a small, simple ground marker for him in Graceland Cemetery in Chicago, Illinois. In 1990 Bob Fitzsimmons was inducted into the International Boxing Hall of Fame.

JAMES J. (JACKSON) JEFFRIES

"The Boilermaker"

B. April 15, 1875 – D. March 3, 1953
Born: Carroll, Ohio
6' 1 ½" / 225 lbs.
Record: 19-1-2 14 KO's (1 NC)

Champion:
June 9, 1899 - May 1905

American born James J. Jeffries was a very athletic man who became known as a "Man among Men" and a "Champion of Champions."

James was a natural athlete excelling as a fast runner and a great high jumper who became very competitive in the sport of Boxing. He remained an amateur until age 20, and as a pro, his style was coined a "brawler" who stayed tucked into a crouched position. James didn't mind taking punishment to get inside of his opponent to beat them down.

As his perfect record continued, James got a title shot on June 9, 1899, in Brooklyn, New York against champion Bob Fitzsimmons. He knocked out the heavy-handed Fitzsimmons in the 11th round at Coney Island, New York to become the 4th gloved and last Heavyweight Champion of the 19th century.

That same year James J. Jefferies toured Europe doing exhibitions and making motion pictures of his bouts. He returned to competition winning a 25-round title defense over a tough Tom Sharkey. James then had a 55 second, 1st round KO over Jack Finnegan, plus winning over ex-Champion Jim Corbett's comeback in the 23rd round.

James agreed to a rematch with ex-Champion Bob Fitzsimmons in 1902 in San Francisco. Fitzsimmons pounded the Champion for eight rounds until James luckily landed a 1-2 combo to KO Fitzsimmons. Next stop in 1903, James hosted ex-Champion "Gentleman Jim" Corbett and controlled him for ten rounds until Corbett's manager threw in the towel.

James had seven title defenses, and in 1905 he retired undefeated, but stayed active in Boxing as a referee and a promoter. However, five years later, he was out of shape, but still tried a comeback on July 4, 1910, in Reno, Nevada against the strong and powerful Jack Johnson. James was guaranteed a sum equivalent to one million dollars today. In the 110° heat, and after 15 rounds, James lost by TKO without ever really having much of a chance.

James retired undefeated in May 1905, and in retirement, built a gym called "Jeffries Barn" which still stands today in Burbank, California.

In 1990, James was inducted into the International Boxing Hall of Fame. Many experts and Boxers believe that James was one of the best Heavyweights of all times.

James J. Jeffries died of a heart attack at age 77 on March 3, 1953, and was buried in Inglewood Park Cemetery in Inglewood, California.

MARVIN HART

"The Louisville Plumber"

B. Sept. 16, 1876 – D. Sept. 17, 1931
Born: Louisville, KY
5' 11 ½" / 195 lbs.
Record: 29-7-4 20 KO's

Champion:
July 3, 1905 - February 23, 1906

American farm boy Marvin Hart got his ring name because his occupation was plumbing. He was also known as the "Fightin' Kentuckian." Marvin was a talented athlete who excelled at wrestling and football in his early years. He didn't begin his Boxing career until 1899 at age 23. His fighting style was very awkward and unorthodox, which made him a tough opponent to read and manage. He was also very aggressive and would take a lot of punishment trying to crowd his opponent and land big blows. The "Plumber" was a powerful puncher with both hands that gave him an additional advantage over his opponents.

As the Louisvillian's record continued, his chances at a title shot increased. In March of 1905 in San Francisco, he stopped the dominant and future Heavyweight Champion, Jack Johnson in 20 rounds. Later that year in July, Marvin got his title shot against former Light Heavyweight Champion, Jack Root in Reno, Nevada. Hart KO'd Root in the 12th round to win the vacated Heavyweight throne by the retired Champion, James J. Jeffries. This victory made Marvin the 5th gloved Heavyweight Champion of the World.

Marvin had one exhibition bout before signing to a title defense against Canadian Tommy Burns in February of 1906 in Los Angeles. The Champ was stopped in the 20th round as Tommy Burns became the new World Heavyweight Champion. Marvin had 12 bouts after winning his title and retired in 1910. He stayed involved with the craft as a Boxing referee. Like many other Boxing celebrities who owned restaurants and bars, Marvin owned a tavern on Market Street in Louisville, Kentucky.

Marvin Hart is the first of four Heavyweight Champions from Louisville, Kentucky that also include: Muhammad Ali, Jimmy Ellis, and Greg Page. Louisville is the first and only other city in the world that has had four Heavyweight World Champions. Incidentally, Ellis, and Page both were at my gym in New Albany, Indiana, for many years.

Marvin Hart died on September 17, 1931, at age 55 of an enlarged liver and high blood pressure. He was laid to rest in the Resthaven Cemetery in Louisville, Kentucky.

TOMMY BURNS

B. June 17, 1881 – D. May 10, 1955
Born: Hanover, Canada
5' 7" / 175 lbs.
Record: 48-5-8 39 KO's

Champion:
February 23, 1905 - December 26, 1908

Tommy Burns has the distinction of being the only Canadian born World Heavyweight Boxing Champion. He was an excellent athlete who played Lacrosse and Hockey in his younger days. He worked several odd jobs before Boxing became his career while in Detroit, Michigan.

Tommy's impressive record mounted, and he earned a title shot six years later in 1906, as an underdog. He met Champion Marvin Hart in Los Angeles, California. The challenger took total command of the bout and stopped the Champion Marvin Hart in the 20th round. With this win, Tommy Burns became the 6th gloved and the shortest World Heavyweight Champion in history, at 5' 7".

Tommy's tenacious, energetic, attacking style with constant footwork, made up for his difference in size. He fought like a middleweight but had the power to punch with the heavyweights.

Tommy was the first World Champion to travel to other countries defending his crown against their National Champions. He made eleven title defenses within three years. Finally, a bigger and stronger contender, Jack Johnson got his title shot at Tommy. Their bout took place in Sydney, Australia on December 26, 1908. It was the largest purse to date giving Tommy $30,000 and Johnson $5,000. Johnson was just too much for the Champion. The police stopped the fight during the 14th round to give Johnson the title.

After a break from Boxing, Tommy went on to win the British Empire title, fought several more times, then retired.

In retirement, Tommy became a Boxing manager, promoter, owned a clothing store, a tavern, and ultimately became an ordained minister in 1948. His life's work made him a wealthy man but lost everything due to the "Great Depression" beginning in 1929.

Tommy Burns died of a heart attack on May 10, 1955, at age 73. Only four people attended his burial at the Ocean View Cemetery in Vancouver, British Columbia, Canada. He was laid to rest in an unmarked grave until a Boxing group came together and gave him a fitting marker. Tommy Burns was inducted into the International Boxing Hall of Fame in 1996.

JACK JOHNSON

"Galveston Giant"

B: March 31, 1878 – D: June 10,
1946 Born: Galveston, TX
6'2"/240 lbs.
Record: 73-13-10 40 KO's (5 NC)

Champion:
December 26, 1908 - April 5, 1915

American Jack Johnson, a "Larger than Life Man,"
became the first African American to win the

Heavyweight Boxing Championship of the World. Jack was the third of nine children to parents who were former slaves. He had limited schooling and dropped out to help support the family in the seaport town of Galveston, Texas.

At the age of 16, Jack moved to New York, but soon returned home to Texas to begin his Boxing career. He took his first fight earning only $1.50. Soon after, he was making around $25.00 per match. Jack was his own man and loved fast living. He was not only a big and strong man, but he also had excellent Boxing skills. He amassed an impressive record, but unfortunately, was avoided by many competitors and Champions.

Jack pursued, and even taunted several current Champions until he finally got his chance at the Heavyweight Crown. On December 26, 1908, in Sydney, Australia, Champion Tommy Burns earned $30,000.00 plus for giving him a shot. Jack dominated the match, and after 14 rounds, it was stopped by the police and declared a TKO, (technical knockout) for Jack, now Champion.

Eventually, promoters planned a big show that was dubbed "The Fight of the Century" on April 5, 1915, for Champion Jack Johnson. His opponent was the Ex-Champion, James J. Jeffries. Jeffries was paid $120,000.00 and Johnson $117.000.00, (both over 3 million today). The grueling bout took place in Reno, Nevada, in 110° sunshine with Jeffries, the 10-7 favorite. The older and out of shape Jeffries couldn't compare to Jack, and the match was declared a TKO after 15 rounds. Jeffries said that he "couldn't beat Johnson one in a thousand times."

After seven years as Champion, Jack took on a much bigger challenger, Jess Willard, at the Oriental Park Race Track in Havana, Cuba. The younger Willard was relentless with body punches that eventually wore down the Champion and knocked him out in the 26th round. Jack fought 12 more years after he lost the title until he was 50 years old. However, he also performed exhibition bouts in many venues, including carnival acts, until the age of 67.

Jack is credited with writing two books and has had countless books, songs, movies, and plays written about him. He is one of the most recognized, respected, and has been considered one of the greatest Boxers of all time.

Jack Johnson was inducted into the Boxing Hall of Fame in 1954 and the International Boxing Hall of Fame in 1990.

Jack Johnson died tragically in an automobile accident in Raleigh, North Carolina, on June 10, 1946, at age 68. He was buried in the Graceland Cemetery in Chicago, Illinois, in an unmarked grave. Later, he received a simple headstone with only "Johnson" on it. The city of Galveston, Texas, dedicated a park and erected a life-size bronze statue of Jack, the seventh World Heavyweight Boxing Champion.

JESS WILLARD

"Pottawatomie Giant"

B. Dec. 29, 1881 – D. Dec. 15, 1968
Born: Pottawatomie, KS
6' 6 ½" / 250 lbs.
Record: 25-7-2 20 KO's

Champion:
April 5, 1915 - July 4, 1919

Midwestern born Jess Willard was from Pottawatomie, Kansas, and was a giant size 6' 6

1/2", 250 pounds "Tower of a Man." However, he was a gentle and friendly person that didn't start Boxing until he was 27 years old. He believed that his size and strength could aid him in making more money in Boxing than any other endeavor, after some failed businesses.

Jess lost his first bout by Disqualification for physically throwing his opponent around the ring. He had incredible strength, stamina, and could withstand tremendous punishment. He was also a powerful and effective counter puncher that could score on his opponent as they attacked or before they could recoil their punches.

Jess's record compiled as he beat the top-ranked Boxers of the time, which earned him a shot at the title. On April 15, 1915, he got his title shot at the 37-year-old Champion Jack Johnson. The match took place at the Oriental Park Race Track in Havana, Cuba. As the hot sun beat down, Johnson seemed to be ahead with his continuous punching to keep Jess away. However, as Johnson punched himself out and absorbed counter punches in the hot sun, a basic 1-2 knockout combo put Johnson down in the 26th round. That combo made Jess Willard the 8th gloved World Heavyweight Champion.

Champion Jess Willard went on to fight several non-title bouts and made one title defense defeating challenger Frank Moran in Madison Square Garden on March 25, 1916.

After four years as Champion, Jess gave a much smaller challenger, Jack Dempsey, a title shot on

Independence Day, July 4, 1919. The 37- year-old Willard met 24 year old Dempsey in Toledo, Ohio, and earned a big payday of $100,000. The bout was very one-sided as Jack Dempsey swarmed the Champion relentlessly and pummeled Jess with seven knockdowns in the 1st round. Jess survived two more rounds but decided not to come out for the fourth round. The Midwestern Jess Willard was very gracious in defeat and congratulated the new World Heavyweight Boxing Champion, Jack Dempsey.

Jess earned a decent living doing exhibitions bouts for the next four years and mounted a comeback on May 12, 1923, taking on Floyd Johnson in Yankee Stadium in New York City. Like the Dempsey fight, he was getting outboxed, but this time he rallied to get in a couple of knockdowns and went on to stop Floyd Johnson with a TKO win.

Jess's next bout was against Argentine Luis Angel Firpo on July 12, 1923, at Boyles Thirty Acres in New Jersey. Seventy-five thousand spectators watched Willard get knocked out in the 8th round. This bout sent the aging Willard into retirement for good.

In retirement, the former World Heavyweight Boxing Champion tried his hand as an actor in a Vaudeville show, Buffalo Bill's Wild West show, and a couple of films. Jess Willard was inducted into the Boxing Hall of Fame in 2003. The "Gentle Giant" died on December 15, 1968, at age 86 of a cerebral hemorrhage. He was laid to rest in Forest Lawn, Hollywood Hills Cemetery in Los Angeles, California.

JACK DEMPSEY

"Manassa Mauler"

B: June 24, 1895 – D: May 31, 1983, Born: Manassa, CO
6' 1"/ 187 lbs.
Record: 54-6-9 44 KO's

Champion:
July 4, 1919 - September 23, 1926

World Heavyweight Boxing Champion, Jack Dempsey, was an American icon equivalent to

Babe Ruth in the 1920s! American William Harrison Dempsey (Jack Dempsey) was born in the Mormon town of Manassa, Colorado, after his parents moved there from West Virginia. William had a religious background who was raised in the Mormon Church. He was a good-natured kid, and at eight years old, took on his first job picking crops to help his family survive. He dropped out of school after the 8th grade and took work as a farmhand, miner, and cowboy. His family moved on to Provo, Utah, when he was 12 years old to be near the manufacturing mines where some decent job opportunities could be found.

William Harrison had an older brother Bernie, who practiced the art of Boxing and became very good. Bernie's way of making money was to work the saloons around Salt Lake City, picking fights as "Jack" Dempsey. Bernie was also teaching little brother William how to box. One day Bernie had one of his scheduled matches but became ill and couldn't compete. Teenage William stepped in using his brother's ring name, "Jack" Dempsey, fought the match, and won. William Harrison Dempsey became known as "Jack" Dempsey from then on.

Jack became an excellent and formidable contestant and at just 17 years old. He traveled to local mining towns also picking fights from 1911 to 1916 as his occupation. To further his career, Jack moved west to San Francisco for more significant opportunities. As his record grew, bigger money fights were being offered to him.

On July 4, 1919, Jack finally got his title shot against the much bigger champion, Jess Willard, in Toledo, Ohio. Surprisingly, Jack mauled Willard and knocked him down seven times in the first round! Willard would only survive two more rounds as he retired on his stool before the fourth round to end the fight early.

That day, Jack Dempsey became the new Lineal World Heavyweight Boxing Champion. He defended his title five times and then met a United States Marine Captain that fought much differently than past opponents.

On September 23, 1926, Jack met "The Fighting Marine," Gene Tunney in Philadelphia, Pennsylvania. Tunney was a crafty, strategic fighter who stayed away from Jack's mauling and aggressive style. Boxing fans were shocked when Tunney outboxed Jack to win a 10-round Decision. Jack asked for a rematch to regain his title that took place a year later in Chicago, Illinois, at Soldier Field on September 22, 1927. Tunney outboxed Jack again but was dropped by Jack in the seventh round. The new rule was to retreat to a neutral corner if your opponent is knocked down. The ten count would not start until the standing Boxer did so. Jack failed to go to the neutral corner immediately in which Tunney had extra time to recover. He did recover and continued to outbox Jack and win a second 10 round Decision to retain his title. The extra time that Tunney got during that knockdown could have cost Jack the crown. This incident became known as "The Long Count" and has actually happened a few times since.

Jack then retired and became a Boxing and Wrestling referee. He also opened a restaurant in New York, acted in a play, and starred in several movies about Boxing. As an author, he wrote several books, including three autobiographies. Jack Dempsey is considered as one of the top ten Heavyweight Boxers of all time. He was inducted into the prestigious "The Ring" Magazine Hall of Fame in 1954 and the International Boxing Hall of Fame in 1990.

It's said as ruthless as he was in the ring, Jack was just as cordial outside the ring. Jack Dempsey died on May 31, 1983, at the age of 87 of heart failure and was laid to rest in Southampton Cemetery, Southampton, New York.

GENE TUNNEY

"The Fighting Marine"

B: May 25, 1897 – D: November 7, 1978
Born: New York, NY
6' 1" / 192 lbs.
Record: 65-1-1 48 KO's

Champion:
September 23, 1926
Retired Undefeated 1928

American Gene Tunney was one of seven children and the last World Heavyweight Champion that was born in the 19th century. Gene began boxing when he was a clerk for The Ocean Steamship Company in New York City when he was still a teenager from 1915 to 1917.

Gene joined the US Marine Corps and eventually was promoted to Captain during WWI. During his service, he won the Light Heavyweight Championship of the American Expeditionary Forces in 1919 in Paris. After he returned home from the service, Gene worked as a lumberjack and in 1922, won the US Light Heavyweight Championship title that he owned until he moved up into the Heavyweight division.

Gene Tunney's Boxing style was very much a scientific and tactical approach that was unlike most, past brawler Champions that would sometimes stand "toe to toe". His style is still emulated by today's Boxers, whose primary goal is to hit without getting hit, behind a consistent jab.

It's believed that Gene had 85 fights all totaled, but his biggest claim to fame was when he beat the world champion, "The Manassa Mauler," Jack Dempsey. They met in Philadelphia on September 23, 1926. Tunney, "The Fighting Marine," shocked the Boxing world as he didn't stand and slug with the "Manassa Mauler." Tunney outboxed Dempsey and won a 10-round Decision to become the new World Heavyweight Champion.

The gracious new Champion agreed to a rematch

a year later in Soldier Field in Chicago, Illinois, September 22, 1927. The second match was a rerun of the first bout until Dempsey caught Gene in the seventh round to put him down on the canvas. The new and agreed rule was that the standing Boxer must go to the neutral corner if your opponent was knocked down. However, Jack did not, therefore giving Tunney more than the ten seconds to regain himself. This is the first incident that is known as "The Long Count." Gene regained composure and continued to outbox Dempsey to retain his crown in 10 rounds.

Gene defended his title one more time against Tom Heeney in 1928. Gene retired without ever been knocked out and only knocked down once by Jack Dempsey in their second bout. He went on to be very successful at manufacturing, insurance, as a bank executive, and at a newspaper.

Gene wrote a couple of books, including an autobiography. He also starred in a movie about himself in 1926 called "The Fighting Marine." He had four children, including John, who became both a US Representative and US Senator from 1971 to 1977.

Gene Tunney was inducted into the World Boxing Hall of Fame in 1980, the International Hall of Fame in 1990, and the US Marine Corp. Hall of Fame in 2001. Gene Tunney died at the age of 81 on November 7, 1978, of a circulation ailment and was laid to rest in Longridge Union Cemetery in Stamford, Connecticut.

MAX SCHMELING

"Black Uhlan of the Rhine"

B: Sept. 28, 1905 D: Feb. 2, 2005
Born: Brandenburg, Germany
6' 1" / 188 lbs.
Record: 56-10-4 40 KO's

Champion:
June 12, 1930 - June 21, 1932

Adolph Otto Siegfried Schmeling was born in
Kleinluckow, Prussia, the German Empire. He

was a son of a sailor/ship navigator. Adolph Otto Siegfried eventually went by the shorter first name of Max. He was a naturally talented athlete in his early years who enjoyed all sports. One day Max viewed a film of the Championship bout between American, Jack Dempsey and Frenchman, Georges Carpentier, and fell in love with Boxing. He began a training program and became a methodical and crafty amateur.

Max's first bout was in 1924 in which he won in his homeland and eventually became the German Champion, then the European Light Heavyweight Champion. After several more wins, Max traveled to America for a bigger chance of success and hired an accomplished Boxing manager, the notable Joe Jacobs. As Jacobs guided him, he accumulated a winning record and was rewarded with a match against one of his Boxing heroes, the tough, Jack Sharkey. The bout took place in the Spring, on Thursday, June 12, 1930, in Yankee Stadium for the title vacated by the retired, Gene Tunney. Sharkey seemed to be controlling the bout until Sharkey fouled Max with a low blow in the fourth round. Max doubled over and appeared unable to continue, causing the referee to award the Heavyweight title to Max on a foul. This decision did not sit well with the Boxing world and consequently was the last Heavyweight Championship title awarded via a foul. A new rule was added after this bout forbidding any Championship being won by a foul.

After this irregular win of the crown, Max moved on with a title defense against a very smooth and accomplished opponent in heavyweight, Young Stribling. They met in The Municipal Stadium in Cleveland, Ohio, on Friday, July 3, 1931. Max won this contest with a TKO after a knockdown at 2:46 in the 15th and last round. Incidentally, Stribling was one of the best Heavyweights ever to enter the ring, but never got his hands on the Championship title...

Interestingly, Young turned pro at 16 years old in high school and compiled a record that was as many as four times the wins of most Champions. Stribling had 253 bouts, (some accounts report 280), with 224 wins and only 13 losses. He was stopped just one time by a TKO, and that was from Max himself. Incredibly, in one-year, Stribling had 55 bouts, which averages more than one a week. He also traveled the world and easily beat many Champions from other countries. Young beat former Champion, Primo Carnera, but lost to ex-Champion, Jack Sharkey, and his title bout with Max Schmeling. His illustrious career consisted of many records that still stand even today. He is credited with the most fights and the most knockouts of any Heavyweight and suffered the fewest knockouts, which was only one TKO by Max, (in which the referee stopped the bout with just 14 seconds left in the fight).

Max graciously gave Jack Sharkey a rematch on Tuesday, June 21, 1932, on Long Island, New York. Again, Sharkey outboxed Max, and this time took the Heavyweight crown in a 15-round Decision. Max never slowed, he went back to the gym to ready himself for his next bout, who was the future Champion, Max

Baer in Yankee Stadium on June 8, 1933. Schmeling's luck did not get better, Baer KO'd him in the 10th round that caused him to drop in the Heavyweight rankings.

However, Max again worked very hard to re-climb the ladder of contention. As he did, opportunity matched him with up and coming, and undefeated Joe Louis on a Friday, June 19, 1936, in Yankee Stadium, in New York City. Max carefully studied fight films of Louis and attended one of his bouts to observe his strengths and weaknesses. Max noted that Louis dropped his hand repeatedly after his jab. He saw that this mistake was ideal for his favorite punch, the right cross. During their meeting, Max proved that his calculation was correct. Max continuously pounded Louis with his robust and accurate right hand until he put him down with a 12th round knockout. It was Louis' first loss, and it bothered him immensely for two years until they could meet again.

In 1935, German Chancellor, Adolf Hitler was excited with his countryman's performance and summoned Schmeling back to Germany aboard the luxurious German airship, the "Hindenburg." Max was met by German leaders, Adolf Hitler and his Generals, who declared Schmeling, a national hero. Hitler saw this as an ideal propaganda opportunity for the "Third Reich". Adolf could show the world that the German race was superior to all others. However, there were some negotiations about Max challenging the current World Champion, American James Braddock, in 1935. Hitler pressured Schmeling to avoid this match in fear of losing the fight to an American with a Jewish manager.

On Tuesday, June 22, 1937, Joe Louis took his shot at the World Heavyweight Champion, James Braddock at Comiskey Park in Chicago. Louis was surprised and knocked down early, but came back to knock out the very game Braddock in the 8th round to become the new World Heavyweight Champion. Even though he was the new Champion, Louis said that he would not feel like the Champion until he beat the one man that beat him, Max Schmeling. Joe Louis got his chance to avenge that loss while Max Schmeling got another shot at the Heavyweight Championship belt on Wednesday, June 22, 1938, in Yankee Stadium. This fight was hailed as the "Fight of the Century," and because of the pre-war world situation, Joe Louis said, "The whole country is depending on me." Joe, now Champion, predicted a second-round knockout. He was wrong; the avenging Louis took the fight to Max from the opening bell with a barrage of punches to quickly KO Max in just one minute and twenty-four seconds of the first round. Max just was not the same adversary as their first match, offering his very defensive posture and style. This match was quite different than their first bout. Max suffered a beating that included bumps, bruises, and two broken ribs, which landed him a two week stay in the hospital. This time Hitler didn't offer Max a luxurious ride on the Hindenburg, but gave him a trip home on a slow steamship that took several days. He was no longer heralded as the hero as before and was even inducted into the German army. Max became a paratrooper, saw action, and was wounded in the "Battle of Crete" in 1941. Later, General Goebbels summoned Max and ordered him to fabricate stories of British abuse of the German prisoners. Max didn't see that, refused to lie, and was court-martialed right away. As time passed, everyone saw that Max was never in agreement with the Hitler regime. He is actually credited with resistance to it by hiding and helping Jewish people, including many children, out of Germany to escape the Nazi's.

After WWll, Max took residence in West Germany and was flat broke. To earn some money, he fought five more times, and after losing his last match, he decided to retire from Boxing at 43 years old. He found work at the Coca-Cola bottling plant in West Germany to earn a living. Like his Boxing career, Max worked his way up the ladder and eventually became the president of the plant and a wealthy man. He also stayed busy doing many interviews, wrote three autobiographies, starred in a movie, and married the beautiful Czechoslovakian movie actress, Anny Ondra.

Following the war, people from enemy countries were allowed as visitors back into the US. In 1954, Max returned to the states, and the American public saw that he was not any part of the German War Machine and greatly defied it. After arriving into the US, he contacted his once opponent, Joe Louis. Max asked to visit him, Joe agreed, and they became terrific friends. Later, when Joe fell on bad financial times, Max happily stepped in and helped him.

The country was saddened when Joe Louis, "The Brown Bomber," and our national hero, died in 1981. At this time, another great friend and famous singer, Frank Sinatra, decided to help with a benefit for Joe's funeral. Max stepped in again and contributed efforts and funds to Joe's service. After Joe's death, Max even sent financial assistance to Joe's widow, and on one occasion, sent a note with the kind words to her, "I didn't only like Joe, I loved him!"

Max was inducted the World Boxing Hall of Fame in 1982 and The International Boxing Hall of Fame in 1991. Max Schmeling died in Wenzendorf, Germany, on Wednesday, February 2, 2005, at 99 years old, making him the oldest former Heavyweight Champion in history. He was laid to rest at Saint Andreas Friedhof Hollenstedt, Landkreis Harburg, Niedersachsen, Germany.

MY OBSERVATION

Max Schmeling was a very cordial and gracious man. He demonstrated that when he was the first person to pick Joe Louis up off the ring canvas after he KO'd him in their first bout. He also immediately rushed to Joe's corner to greet him, like old friends, when he entered the ring before their second bout!

Max had a very defensive style of fighting and was an apprehensive counter puncher. He was a patient

Boxer that would try to find his opponent's weakness and would take advantage of lucky shots. He would use this advantage and become very aggressive when he had his opponent hurt. Max was usually a good finisher.

This defensive style will work against some Boxers, but not all. It will not necessarily work on the same opponent every time. For instance, it worked on Joe Louis during the first meeting, but not in their second.

The disadvantage of this defensive style is that the Boxer's energy and motion is regressing from the opponent much of the time, while the opponent's energy is going forward. Accurate punching and the ability to avoid punches from the opponent will also add to the defensive Boxer's problems.

Therefore, the Boxer, who can switch from a defensive style to an advancing attacker as needed, is the ultimate Boxer. However, usually, a Boxer has one style that he's better at, and switching is not easy for them. Roy Jones, Sugar Ray Robinson, Muhammad Ali, Sugar Ray Leonard, and Floyd Mayweather are prime examples of Boxers who could switch from the very defensive fighter to a vicious attacker and finisher.

Max was the longest living former World Heavyweight Champion who died at 99 years old. So, just maybe, the defensive fighting style was the best one for Max!

JACK SHARKEY

Joseph Paul Zukauskas

B: Oct. 26, 1902 D: Aug. 17, 1994
Born: Binghampton, New York
Record: 38-14-3 13 KO's
6' 1" / 205 lbs.

Champion:
June 21, 1932 - June 29, 1933

American Joseph Paul Zukauskas was the son
of Lithuanian immigrants who settled into

Binghampton, New York. Joseph served in the US Navy during WWI, where he learned to box and became the Atlantic Fleet Champion. After the war, he decided to change his ring name to "Jack Sharkey." He took first name "Jack" from his favorite 1920's revered Boxing icon, Jack Dempsey. He took the last name as "Sharkey," after another tough Boxing, US Navy sailor, Tom Sharkey, who fought Champion James J. Jeffries twice. The new "Jack Sharkey" turned pro in 1924, winning his very first bout and only lost three times in the next three years.

Jack Sharkey became a skillful and powerful Boxer who was a top contender that fought many other competitors and Champions of the day. He fought the big names around like Joe Louis, Primo Carnera, Max Schmeling, and even his idol, Jack Dempsey.

Jack Sharkey ultimately was paired against Jack Dempsey, the man that he deeply admired, on Tuesday, June 14, 1927, at Yankee Stadium, in New York. The winner of this bout would be in line to receive a Championship title fight with the Champion, Gene Tunney. To his surprise, he was winning against Dempsey when he believed he was fouled by a low blow. He turned to complain to the referee with his hands down, and Dempsey clocked him with a left hook that KO'd him; incidentally, the referee's last-minute instruction is "protect yourself at all times." However, this silly mistake has happened several other times in Boxing history!

A year before, Gene Tunney challenged Jack Dempsey

for the Championship on Thursday, September 23, 1926, at Sesquicentennial Stadium in Philadelphia, Pennsylvania. Here Gene won an unbelievable, 15 round Decision. Tunney offered Dempsey a rematch one year later on Thursday, September 22, 1927, at Soldier's Field in Chicago, Illinois. This bout became known as "The Long Count" as Dempsey dropped Tunney but wouldn't immediately return to the neutral corner. This gave Tunney extra time to regain his senses. Tunney was able to recover and continued outboxing Dempsey to retain his title. Tunney retired with only one loss and left the Heavyweight throne open.

This gave Jack an opportunity to fight for the crown. His opponent was German Max Schmeling. On Thursday, June 12, 1930, Jack was doing well and seemed to be winning until he caught Schmeling with a low blow that dropped him to his knees in pain. Things were so confusing and chaotic that the some of the officials pressed the referee to disqualify Jack by a foul. He did and this gave Max Schmeling the new World Heavyweight Boxing Title. However, after this bout, the rules were changed so that no Championship Title could be won via a foul. In addition, all Boxers must now wear a boxing cup supporter during the bout.

Jack's next bout was against a gigantic man and future Champion, Italian, Primo Carnera, on Monday, October 12, 1931. The elusive Jack Sharkey won this meeting by a Unanimous Decision in their 15-round affair in Madison Square Garden. Even though Carnera was a giant of 6' 6" and 245 pounds, Jack wisely avoided his power.

Jack's record earned him another shot at the title when he was matched up again against Max Schmeling, the current Champion. On Tuesday, June 21, 1932, at New York's Long Island Bowl. Jack's dream was realized when he won on a Decision to finally grasp the World Heavyweight Boxing Title Belt.

The next year, the new Champion gave a previous competitor, Primo Carnera, a shot at his title on Thursday, June 29, 1933, in Madison Square Garden. Jack felt he could pull off another win over him and was outboxing Carnera again until an uppercut from nowhere slipped in to knock him out in the 6th round. This made Primo Carnera the new and first World Heavyweight Boxing Champion from Italy.

Jack's career slowed, and he was matched against the sensational, Joe Louis, known as "The Brown Bomber," on August 18, 1936, in Philadelphia. Jack was visibly past his prime as Louis took charge and dropped the 34-year-old Jack four times before knocking him out in the third round which sent him into retirement... incidentally, Jack Sharkey is the only man to fight the two the Boxing greats, Jack Dempsey of the 1920s and Joe Louis of the 1930s and 1940s.

Jack continued to stay around the ring as he became a Boxing and Wrestling referee while also doing some personal appearances. He was also inducted into the International Boxing Hall of Fame in 1994.

Like many other Boxing Champions, Jack tried his hand at business which included a bar in Boston, Massachusetts.

Jack Sharkey died Wednesday, August 17, 1994, at the age of 91, which made him one of the oldest former Heavyweight Champions in history. He passed from respiratory arrest and was buried in Prospect Cemetery in Epping, New Hampshire.

MY OBSERVATION

Jack Sharkey was a very likable man and a naturally talented athlete with good footwork in the ring. He was a skillful Boxer with quick hands and a very effective jab. He could fight from the outside or rough it up on the inside.

I believe Jack could have easily competed with today's best Boxer's. He fought the best contenders and Champions of his day and earned his spot on the list of great World Boxing Champions!

PRIMO CARNERA

"The Ambling Alp"
B: October 26, 1906 D: June 29, 1967
Born: Sequals, Italy
6' 6" / 275 lbs.
Record: 89-14-0 72 KO's
"Over 50 KO Club"

Champion:
June 29, 1933 - June 14, 1934

Italian born Primo Carnera was an exceptionally large human from the beginning as he weighed 22 pounds at birth. He was born to a stone cutter family that lived in a tiny town in Northeastern Italy. By age eight, Primo was the size of a full-grown man, and around this time, his family picked up and moved to France.

Primo was an easy-going person who was very likable and kind to everyone that he met. As a young person, he reluctantly joined a traveling circus as a freak show giant. He also wrestled in the show to earn some extra money. Although he enjoyed the physical contact and the sport of Wrestling, he wanted to earn more. So, he picked up odd jobs to make ends meet. He would soon find out that Boxing paid a lot more money.

While drifting around Paris, Frenchman Boxer, Paul Journee spotted Primo as he was broke and basically homeless on a park bench. Journee thought that Primo's size would be unique and exciting in the world of Boxing. Journee then introduced him to a local Boxing manager, Leon See. Primo began training with See and quickly collected a winning 16-2 record in France. In 1930, with his winning record, Primo Carnera and his manager believed it was time to move on to the United States. They hired an additional manager, Walter Friedman, to their group. The future looked very bright as his managers believed that Primo would be successful as the American public would love to see a man of such size in the ring. It's also reported Friedman and See were not so fair with Primo's earnings.

After working and winning more bouts, a few by questionable decisions, Primo was able to challenge the future champion, Jack Sharkey. Sharkey outboxed him, but Primo went the distance and lost in a 10-round show on October 12, 1931. After this loss, Primo went on a European tour flattening most of his overmatched opponents.

Next, Primo returned to New York and added more victims to his record. He eventually earned the right to fight again for the Heavyweight title. It happened to be a prior opponent, now the Heavyweight Champion, Jack Sharkey.

The fight was scheduled for Thursday, June 29, 1933, in Madison Square Garden, New York. Primo, the much taller and heavier opponent, was being outboxed again, but unexpectedly, KO'd the much smaller Sharkey in the sixth round with an uppercut that he never saw coming. With this victory, Primo Carnera became the first Italian to win the "Lineal" World Heavyweight crown. Primo then won two title defenses, first against Spain's, Paolino Uzcudun in a 15-round decision on October 22, 1933. Next, against former Light Heavyweight Champion, Tommy Loughran in a 15-round decision on March 1, 1934.

Primo, now the World Champion, was challenged by the wild swinging, and heavy-hitting Max Baer. When they met on June 14, 1934, Primo was outboxed at the beginning of the bout, then started doing a little better in the late; however, after being floored 11 times, he lost as the referee stopped the fight. The referee awarded Max Baer the Heavyweight Title by TKO in the 11th round at the Madison Square Garden Bowl in Long Island, New York.

Primo got back in the ring touring South America and won several more bouts. Another big chance came his way when he landed a match with Boxing sensation, Joe Louis. The fight took place on Tuesday, June 25, 1935, in Yankee Stadium in New York. Louis simply had no trouble outboxing Primo and ultimately knocked him out in the 6th round. Primo said that Louis was the best opponent that he had ever met in the ring.

Primo again didn't give up and continued to work his craft, making good paydays. Although he earned a great amount of money throughout his career, his managers seemed to end up with more of the winnings. Therefore, needing to earn more money, back on the road, Primo went. He took on eight more bouts, winning five and losing three. Nearing 40 years old, he decided to retire from Boxing altogether.

Primo wanted to stay active and earn money, so he thought he could make a living at something that he was very good at. So, he decided to return to his old profession, Wrestling. In 1946 Primo joined the world of Professional Wrestling and won several national and international titles. He amassed a remarkable record of 143-1-1, which is very impressive, winning almost every match that he fought. He defeated the former World Champion, Ed "Strangler" Lewis, but just before he retired, couldn't overcome the current

Champion, Lou Thesz, in May 1948. Very few men in history have had the talents to accumulate a winning record in Boxing and Wrestling!

Primo Carnera is the first to be included in the exclusive "Over 50 Knock Out Club" with 72 knockouts in his Boxing career. He was multi-talented and moved on to a movie career appearing in over 15 films as a big box office draw in American and Italian successes. He was always ranked high in "The Ring" magazine credits, ranked as a high contender, and was on its cover in 1931.

Primo became an American citizen in 1953 and settled in Los Angeles, California where he opened a restaurant and liquor store. Carnera died of Liver disease and diabetes in Sequals, Italy, on Thursday, June 29, 1967, at age 60. He was laid to rest in the Carnera Family Plot in Sequals, Provincia di Pordenone, Friuli-Venezia Giulia, Italy.

MY OBSERVATION

Primo Carnera was a passive personality and trusting person who became a Champion of Boxing and Wrestling. The typical process was for the managers to handle the earnings and bookkeeping. It's reported that some of his team members took great advantage of his trust and his earnings.

Primo was commonly accused of being clumsy and lacked talent. He was referred to as "The Ambling Alp," meaning he lacked balance and body control. I watched his bouts, and he was a little awkward, and his footwork was not correct. He lacked finesse and made some mistakes that I would blame on his trainers. They should have made him more calculating, mechanical, and controlled in his approach.

Primo's size, 6'6" and 245 lbs., meant that he had the advantage of size, but would have to be aware of some basic physics. A Boxer who is that much taller naturally has the reach advantage with longer arms and bigger steps. However, he is punching downward with gravity that can easily throw him off balance. This Boxer must be careful not to over-reach or over-commit to avoid the shorter counter puncher. He should keep feet farther apart and appropriately take shorter steps. Also, continuously use his filling, feeling, and insurance jabs. These quick, recoiling jabs will also conserve energy needed in the later rounds that many times belong to the shorter opponent. Primo may have been a little awkward in Boxing but did well in Wrestling. He accumulated a 143-1-1 wrestling record and won many championships after he retired from Boxing which is very, very impressive!

MAX BAER

B: Feb. 11, 1909 D: Nov. 21, 1959
Born: Omaha, Nebraska
6' 2" / 210 lbs.
Record 71-13-0 59 KO's
"Over 50 KO Club"

Champion:
June 14, 1934 - June 13, 1935

Maximilian Adelbert Baer was born in America's Midwest to the German/Jewish father, Jacob Baer, and Mother Dora Bales of Scottish and Irish descent. The family moved from Omaha, Nebraska to Durango, Colorado, then on to Alameda, California, in 1922. Max's father became a butcher around the San Francisco area and got Max a job as a delivery boy when he was just a youngster. Max eventually became a butcher boy and picked up other jobs that helped him develop the extra strength that ultimately made him a powerful puncher. He also signed up for the famous "Charles Atlas" bodybuilding course that added even greater body strength.

Max picked up on Boxing, trained hard, and turned pro in 1929. The very next year, he fought for the Pacific Coast Championship against a tough Frankie Campbell. Under extraordinary and strange circumstances, Max's friend and trainer switched to his opponent's camp the very night before their bout. To make things worse, his trainer who betrayed him, taunted and jeered him from the opposite corner during the entire fight. As the match ensued, Campbell hit Max that caused a flash knockdown, which had little effect. Thinking that he had really hurt Max, Campbell turned to the crowd to receive cheers and acclaim. However, Max sprang up and slugged Campbell, stunning him, then continued to pound him until the referee stopped the fight. Shockingly, Campbell died the very next day. Max was charged with manslaughter, but was acquitted of charges due to the coroner's report. The report stated that all punches were legal ones inside the ring. Even with this exoneration, Max was sad, distraught, and considered never boxing again. However, after some coaxing and consideration, he did continue boxing, but graciously gave his purses for several bouts to the Campbell family.

As Max eventually began training again, he took on his next opponent, Ernie Schaaf, on Friday, September 19, 1930, in Madison Square Garden, New York. Max gave Schaaf great punishment throughout the fight, and then KO'd him at the bell in the last round. It took three full minutes to revive Schaaf, but then he seemed to be all right. However, Schaaf immediately complained of constant headaches in the following months. Schaaf continued his training and took on his next bout with the ex-Champion, Primo Carnera. Carnera struck Schaaf with a single jab, and he went down hard. Schaaf died shortly afterwards. The original speculation was that his death was the effects of the Baer bout. However, the medical results showed that Ernie Schaaf's demise was caused by a case of influenza and meningitis.

Max then signed to a contest with the German-born Max Schmeling on Thursday, June 8, 1933, in Yankee Stadium, New York. Schmeling's defensive style was just not workable against the stronger Baer. Max Baer beat the former Heavyweight Champion, Max Schmeling, by winning a TKO in the 10th round. The accumulation of these bouts finally brought Baer to Madison Square Garden on Thursday, June 14, 1934, challenging the current Champion, Primo Carnera. Max's punching power and boxing skills were too much for Carnera as he dropped him eleven times before winning the fight by a TKO in the 11th round. Max Baer was now the new lineal World Heavyweight Boxing Champion.

Max held the title for 364 days as he met 8 to 1 underdog, James J. Braddock in Long Island, New York. Max hardly trained as he took Braddock as an easy challenger while Braddock trained very fiercely for this bout. As the fight got underway, Max joked and clowned around at the beginning of the match until he started getting hit repeatedly. Max began to settle down and show serious attempts of landing some hard punches, but it was too little, too late. Not enough of them landed, and due to lack of training, he began to tire. Max lost this 15-round Unanimous Decision and saw his opponent, James J. Braddock, become the new World Heavyweight Boxing Champion. James Braddock then became widely known as the "Cinderella Man" in which, incidentally, 71 years later in 2005, a movie about James and his career was made.

Three months later, on September 24, 1935, Max Baer found himself in the ring with the undefeated "Brown Bomber," Joe Louis,... Max was outmatched. He was knocked to one knee in the 2nd round, knocked down in the 4th round, and with no chance to continue, the referee stopped the bout and gave Louis the win. Joe Louis was moving closer to his Heavyweight Championship bout.

Toward the end of Max's career, he fought Lou Nova on June 1, 1939, in the very first televised Boxing match on New York WNBT-TV, where he lost. Max met Nova again on Friday, April 4, 1941, where he lost again by a TKO in the 8th round.

Max Baer was ranked as number 20 in the 50 greatest Heavyweights of all time. He is also in the "Over 50 Knock Out Club" with 59 KO's. Max was inducted into the Boxing Hall of Fame in 1968, The World Boxing Hall of Fame in 1984, The International Hall of Fame in 1995, and The International Jewish Hall of Fame in 2009.

In retirement, Max worked as a Boxing and Wrestling referee like many retired Boxers and Wrestlers. Max also worked as a disc jockey on a Sacramento radio station, had his own TV variety show, and acted in 20 movies. He had a brother who was also an accomplished Boxer, Buddy Baer. Max was the father of Max Baer Jr., who played "Jethro Bodine" on the 1960's TV series, "The Beverly Hillbillies."

Max Baer died of a heart attack at the age of only 50 years old on Thursday, June 13, 1935. He was laid to rest in St. Mary's Catholic Cemetery in Sacramento, California, where over 1500 people attended his funeral.

MY OBSERVATION

Max Baer was a strong athlete with unusual upper body strength. I thought that he was a better than average fighter for the era. He was more of a slugger, wailer, and brawler than a Boxer.

Max didn't seem to choose finesse, but liked to rush into his opponent. He wanted to use a series of punches to get his opponent moving backwards then, he liked to use right overhands to club his opponents. I believe that he carried his hands too low and punched from his hips too much, which made him susceptible to a good jab.

This common style of the time worked well for him until his bout with "The Brown Bomber," Joe Louis, on September 24, 1935. Louis displayed the ultimate in Boxing skills with effective jabs, right crosses, hooks, uppercuts, and overhands, all landing on Max that night. Louis' defensive abilities were also an advantage to nullify Max's brawling style.

JAMES J. BRADDOCK

"Cinderella Man"

B: June 8, 1905 D: November 29, 1974
Born: New York City, NY
6' 2" / 195 lbs.
Record 51-26-7-2 25 KO's

Champion:
June 13, 1935 - June 22, 1937

James Walter Braddock was one of seven children born on W. 48th St, in Hell's Kitchen located in New

York City. His parents were Anglo/Irish Immigrants, Joseph Braddock, and Elizabeth O'Toole Braddock. The family moved over to New Jersey when James was a youngster. James had his future sights set on playing football at Notre Dame University after high school.

James didn't play football at Notre Dame, but discovered Boxing as a teenager. He quickly developed a successful amateur career and turned pro at 21 years old as a Light Heavyweight. His first fight was in November 1923, and like most of his wins, this was an early-round KO.

In three years, James compiled a 42-2-2 record with 25 KO's. He was a great counter puncher, had a great right hand, and could take a punch.

James got married, and with three young kids, his responsibilities grew. He eventually got a shot at the Light Heavyweight title, but couldn't get the win. Shortly after that, the "Great Depression" hit America on "Black Thursday," October 24, 1929.

As the economy took a dive, so did James' career. He lost 16 of his next 22 fights and broke one of his fragile hands. Since his Boxing career was not doing so well, James stopped boxing and took on odd jobs to survive. He worked the shipping docks and even shoveled snow to feed his family. However, it wasn't enough, so the proud James Braddock, had to reluctantly take on government assistance just to feed his family.

As James worked regular jobs, he didn't give up on his passion for Boxing. He thought that he would just use this downtime to get in better shape and let his hands heal. They did heal, and he started taking on new bouts. He began winning again and got some renewed attention. One day, James got a call as there was cancellation on the undercard of a Max Baer Championship title bout.

He was expected to lose, but won a 3rd round KO over the journeyman, John Griffin. This win got him another key bout with another tough opponent, John Henry Lewis. Again, James was the underdog, and again he won a 10-round victory to surprise the Boxing promoters. The wins kept coming as James met veteran Art Lasky and won in 15 rounds.

The current champion, Max Baer decided James would be an easy title defense and put him on the card on Thursday, June 13, 1935, in Madison Square Garden, New York. James was an 8 to 1 underdog; therefore, Baer did little training to prepare for the fight. However, James studied Baer's style and was aware of his strength and his powerful right hand. James also trained extremely hard and said that this bout would be nothing compared to what he had endured the past few years.

This night belonged to James J. Braddock. Baer thought his skills and talent would take the challenger out easily. Baer played and clowned while James was very serious and got down to business from the opening bell. James methodically and consistently attacked the Champion until James was unbelievably awarded the 15-round Unanimous Decision and the new Lineal World Heavyweight Boxing Championship Title.

James then became widely known as the "Cinderella Man" as this bout was considered the biggest upset since John L. Sullivan lost to "Gentleman" James Corbett on Wednesday, September 7, 1892, in New Orleans, Louisiana.

James J. Braddock was a man of character, pride and principles. He was moved to return all the government money and assistance that he had been given to him when he was struggling in his bad financial times. In addition, James also began making donations to underprivileged families in various assistance programs.

James took on challenger Joe Louis on Tuesday, June 22, 1937, at Comiskey Park in Chicago, Illinois. James did very well, considering that he was taking medication for arthritis in his hands. It's reported that the medication could have caused him to be little sluggish and a somewhat slower. However, James knocked Louis down early and held his own, but was just not in the condition to last, and lost by KO in the 8th round. This meeting declared Joe Louis the new World Heavyweight Boxing Champion.

However, James and his manager did negotiate a unique and unbelievable deal with the challenger, Joe Louis. Their contract gave James 10% of Joe's purse for the next ten years. James collected a terrific amount of $150,000 in just the first two years.

The proud James J. Braddock wanted to go out on top before he retired. Therefore, he took one last bout against Tommy Farr on Friday, January 21, 1938.

James won this last competition by a Split Decision in 10 rounds.

In 1942, during WWll, James enlisted into the US Army, was promoted to the rank of 1st lieutenant, and was stationed on the island of Saipan. He was assigned to teach fellow service members hand to hand combat due to his experience and expertise. After the war, James returned home to his family and normal life.

James was inducted into "The Ring" Hall of Fame in 1964, the Hudson County Hall of Fame in 1991, and the International Hall of Fame in 2001. In 2005, Ron Howard directed a hit movie titled "Cinderella Man," covering James' life and career that was played by actor Russell Crowe.

James J. Braddock died peacefully in his sleep on Friday, November 29, 1974, at the age of 69. He was laid to rest in Mount Carmel Cemetery in Tenafly, New Jersey.

MY OBSERVATION

James J. Braddock was a man of character and integrity who lived through the 1930's Depression-era. He was an excellent Boxer who had a fast jab, an effective overhand punch, and was a quick counter puncher. He was also a very mechanical and methodical Boxer who was good at offense and defense.

In June 1937, "The Cinderella Man" gave Joe Louis, a sensational Boxer, all that he could handle until the 6th round of their Championship bout. James began to slow, and consequently, Joe landed a big right hand that KO'd him in the 8th round. It was later learned that James was on some medication for his arthritis that could have contributed to his slowing.

James J. Braddock was a credit to the Boxing world, and I enjoyed watching him work!

JOE LOUIS

"The Brown Bomber"

B: May 13, 1914 D: April 12, 1981
Born: Lafayette, Alabama
6' 2" / 195 lbs.
Record: 66-3 52 KO's
"Over 50 KO Club"

Champion:
June 22, 1937 - March 1, 1949

Joseph Louis Barrow was a shy and quiet kid who was one of eight children born into a poor Alabama family. His parents were sharecroppers, and he was a grandson of slaves from the deep South. Joseph lost his father when he was young, and after some time, his mother remarried and moved to Detroit, Michigan.

Joe's mother wanted the best for Joe and gave him extra money that she saved for violin lessons. However, when a friend introduced him to a local Boxing gym, he took a path in a much different direction. He secretly began taking the violin lessons money and used it for Boxing. He also took on some odd jobs to support his new interest. He then started his amateur career using the ring name "Joe Louis." He left off his last name thinking his mother wouldn't find out that he was boxing and become upset.

Naturally, Joe's mother eventually found out about his Boxing as his amateur career soared to 50 wins in 54 bouts with 43 KOs. He also became the 1934 Detroit Golden Gloves Heavyweight Champion and won the United States AAU Championship title in St. Louis, Missouri.

Joe began his professional career on Wednesday, July 4, 1934, with a first-round knockout of his opponent, Jack Kracken. He remained undefeated until an upset Knockout loss to Germany's Max Schmeling on Monday, June 22, 1936, in Yankee Stadium, New York. Schmeling wisely studied Joe's style, strengths, and weaknesses. Max saw that Joe had one little mistake, he dropped his hand low after every jab. Max knew what to do. He took advantage of this mistake and countered Joe's jab with his powerful right cross repeatedly until he was victorious with a 12th round KO.

Joe would meet Schmeling again when he was the Heavyweight Champion. One year later, three years after turning pro, Joe got a chance to challenge the Heavyweight Champion, James J. Braddock, "The Cinderella Man." On Tuesday, June 22, 1937, the fight was on at Madison Square Garden, New York. Braddock knocked Joe down to begin the fight, but as Joe settled down and rallied, he outboxed Braddock to finish with an 8th round knockout. Joe Louis, "The Brown Bomber," became the new World Heavyweight Boxing King for the next 12 years. His reign is the longest even to today.

Joe fought "all-comers" during his reign, including the day's top Boxers and many journeymen. He had 25 title defenses and fought club fighters plus the past and future Champions. Joe took on the likes of Primo Carnera, Max Baer, Buddy Baer, Jack Sharkey, Ezzard Charles, "Jersey" Joe Walcott, Max Schmeling, Billy Conn, and Lee Savold, beating most of them by knockout. Only three men were able to beat Joe in 69 bouts, Max Schmeling, Ezzard Charles, and Rocky Marciano. Yes, he was surprised by Schmeling earlier in his career, but lost only to Charles and Marciano after his prime. He returned after nearly a two-year retirement for financial reasons and was closing in on the age of forty.

Joe was hailed as a national hero when he was matched against Germany's Max Schmeling during the period that Adolf Hitler was ramping up his sites on world domination. He had lost to Schmeling on Friday, June 19, 1936, at Yankee Stadium, but got this rematch in June 1938. This bout was touted by promoters as "The Fight of the Century." Joe had been waiting for this rematch for two years and said he wouldn't feel like the Champion until he beat the one man that had beaten him. Joe jumped Max from the first bell, and in 124 seconds, KO'd the past Champion to redeem himself, and earn the victory that made him feel like the true Champion.

Joe joined the US Army during WWll and was eventually promoted to the rank of sergeant and served with a great friend and another American hero, Brooklyn Dodger, Jackie Robinson. Joe fought 96 exhibitions for the Armed Forces morale and donated $100,000 to the Army and Navy relief funds. He could only defend his title three times in four years between 1942 through 1945 during the war. After the war, Joe fought and won twice in 1946, once in 1947, and his last bout against "Jersey" Joe Walcott in 1948.

Joe retired on March 1, 1949 and had earned four and one half million dollars during his career. However, he developed financial problems due to divorces, donations, careless spending, legal issues, and a tax debt. These financial woes forced him back into the ring after a short retirement.

At age 36, on Wednesday, September 27, 1950,

older and rusty Joe Louis returned to the ring to meet Ezzard Charles to help pay his debts. Joe lasted but lost a 15-round Decision on his comeback attempt. However, Joe won his next eight bouts then, signed to fight the undefeated, Rocky Marciano on Friday, October 26, 1951. It was clear from the beginning that he was not the tuned, Joe Louis of the 1930s and 1940s. Joe was stopped in the 8th round by a TKO and suffered the third loss of his career, which retired him for good this time.

Joe continued his passion by trying his hand at Wrestling, plus refereed Wrestling and Boxing matches as some retired Boxers did before him. Joe did other extra jobs to help earn a living, including a celebrity greeter for Caesar's Palace in Las Vegas. In Joe's later years, Las Vegas singer, Frank Sinatra and Joe became good friends. Frank gladly helped Joe cope with some of his personal concerns.

There is a seven-foot statue in Caesars Palace of Joe who greeted so many of their customers over the years. There is also another statue of him in his hometown of Detroit, Michigan that was erected in 1986. He is included in the "Over 50 Knockout Club," he was inducted into "The Ring" magazine Hall of Fame in 1954, and the International Boxing Hall of Fame in 1990. Joe was posthumously awarded the Congressional Gold Medal in 1982 and was the first Boxer featured on a U.S. commemorative postage stamp. There was a movie made about our national hero, titled "The Joe Louis Story," in 1953.

Joe developed heart problems and in 1977 had heart surgery. As time passed, he became confined to a wheelchair.

Frank Sinatra helped Joe Louis for the next four years live gracefully until he passed away from cardiac arrest at the Desert Springs Hospital Medical Center in Las Vegas Valley, Nevada, on Sunday, April 12, 1981, at age 66. He was laid to rest as a hero in Arlington National Cemetery in Arlington, Virginia.

MY OBSERVATION

Joe Louis was a soft-spoken and humble man that held the Heavyweight crown longer than any other man from June 1937 to March 1949.

I watched Joe's bouts and was impressed with his very smooth, methodical, and robotic performances. He was a naturally talented Boxer who seemed to do a lot of damage with minimal effort. He was also proficient with every type of punch in his arsenal, scoring on opponents at will. Joe's style would fall under the term "Boxer." He had a calculating offense that used all punches proficiently. He also had competent defensive skills in which he would stay away from his opponent and use the ring space to his advantage. Some notable "Boxers" of this style were Muhammad Ali, Evander Holyfield, Riddick Bowe, and Lennox Lewis.

The shorter man is usually the inside fighter and typically is called a "slugger," "brawler," "mauler," or "swarmer." This fighter wants to slip the taller opponent's long arms, get inside, and do damage to the body. The notable inside fighters are Jack Dempsey, Rocky Marciano, Joe Frazier, and Mike Tyson.

There are two fighting stances for Boxers to use. Most of the fighters use the "Orthodox" stance in which he faces his opponent with the left-hand lead. The "Southpaw" faces with his right hand forward and right foot forward. Joe Louis used the "Orthodox" stance.

Joe was also America's hero during the WWll era and who my Dad still talks about today. My Dad is 93 years old and started Boxing in the Navy during WWll, like many other service members. Joe boosted morale for the servicemen on the front lines during the war. Joe Louis is indeed an American icon and hero, and he's one of my top three favorite Heavyweights!

EZZARD MACK CHARLES

"Cincinnati Cobra"

B: July 7, 1921 D: May28, 1975
Born: Lawrenceville, Georgia
6' 0" / 201 lbs.
Record: 96-25-1 52 KO's
"Over 50 KO Club"

Champion:
September 27, 1950 - July 18, 1951

Ezzard Mack Charles was born in Lawrenceville, Georgia, but moved to Cincinnati, Ohio, to live with his grandmother when he was a youngster. As a teenager, he attended Woodward High School and became interested in Boxing there. He had natural talent and trained diligently to win the Golden Gloves Welterweight title in 1938 and the Golden Gloves Middleweight National title in 1939 with a perfect 42-0 record.

Ezzard turned pro in 1940 and beat all twelve opponents that he faced. He only lost one Decision of nine bouts in 1941, and only lost one Decision in twelve bouts during 1942.

Ezzard joined the US Military during WWll and only had a few bouts during those years as he settled into the Light Heavyweight division. After the war, in 1946, he compiled a long string of wins while climbing the ladder to a Heavyweight title shot.

On Wednesday, June 22, 1949, Ezzard met future World Champion, Jersey Joe Walcott, for the National Boxing Association title that was left open by the retired champion, Joe Louis. Ezzard beat Jersey Joe in this matchup and they would face each other three more times. On Friday, September 22, 1950, in Yankee Stadium, Ezzard won a Decision over iconic and ex-Champion, Joe Louis, who was returning to the ring from retirement. This bout was justification for him to become recognized as the true and Lineal World Heavyweight Champion. (Charles had out punched Walcott to win the vacant interim crown). Ezzard faced Walcott in a rematch on Wednesday, March 7, 1951, and won again with a Unanimous Decision in 15 rounds. Ezzard defended his title eight times and then met Jersey Joe in their "rubber match" that occurred for the third time on Wednesday, July 18, 1951. Ezzard was not so lucky this time. Walcott knocked out the Champ in the 7th round to take the World Heavyweight Boxing Championship belt. Ezzard had a fourth and final bout with Walcottt in efforts to regain the Championship from the Heavyweight Champ. Ezzard lost the controversial 15-round Unanimous Decision on Thursday, June 5, 1952. If Ezzard had won this bout, he would have been the first man to regain the Heavyweight title.

Ezzard Charles wasn't going to give up. He had fourteen more bouts as he worked himself back into contention for another title shot. Through an elimination series, he was able to challenge the reigning Champion and unbeaten, Rocky Marciano, on Thursday, June 17, 1954. Ezzard displayed his excellent ring savvy, worked as hard as Rocky, but wasn't awarded the win. He lost by a 15 round controversial Decision. Many were very angry and thought that Ezzard had won this fight. To Ezzard's credit, he is the only man to last 15 rounds with Rocky Marciano. However, Rocky did give Ezzard a rematch on Friday, September 17, 1954. Ezzard was giving as good as he got and caught Rocky with a punch that split Rocky's nose in half in the 6th round. Rocky's corner could not stop the bleeding, and the referee was seriously considering a halt to the bout in the 7th round. Rocky pleaded for one more round. The referee agreed, and the 8th round continued with Ezzard and Rocky trading punches, and then it happened. They both were throwing knockout punches in the 8th round, when Rocky caught Ezzard with his explosive right hook...it was the knockout of a lifetime.

Due to financial concerns, Ezzard continued to fight for 23 more bouts, but only won ten of them. He wanted to go out on top and finally retired after his Unanimous Decision win in December 1955 over Toxie Hall.

Ezzard got his nickname, the "Cincinnati Cobra" because his jabs were so quick, and he had explosive combinations. He was a very skilled and talented Boxer that has been rated as one of the greatest Light Heavyweight Champions of all time. He also beat many Hall of Famers in three different weight classes.

Ezzard Charles is also included into the "Over 50 Knockout Club", was inducted into "The Ring" magazine Boxing Hall of Fame in 1970, and The International Boxing Hall of Fame in 1990. He was also named one of the greatest fighters of all time by "The Ring" magazine, International Boxing Research Organization, and "The ESPN Boxing Magazine."

Ezzard was featured on a 1949 U.S. commemorative stamp as the World Heavyweight Champion and has a street named for him in his hometown of Cincinnati, Ohio.

In retirement, he tried his hand at acting as he

starred in the movie, "Mau Drums" in 1960. He was also musically inclined as he played the double bass with some jazz bands around town. Ezzard maintained a close friendship with Rocky Marciano and was also a friend and neighbor of Muhammad Ali when they lived in Chicago.

Ezzard Charles was diagnosed with ALS in 1968 that ultimately left him completely disabled and in a wheelchair. Ezzard Charles died in a nursing home on Wednesday, May 28, 1975, at age 53. He was laid to rest in Burr Oak Cemetery, Alsip, Cook County, Illinois.

MY OBSERVATION

Ezzard Charles was a naturally talented fighter who started Boxing as a teenager.

I watched Ezzard's bouts and saw his quick jab and his hard punches that allowed him to fight on the outside or brawl with body punches on the inside. He worked with a complete arsenal of punches and was effective with all of them.

I was impressed with as Ezzard as he was a Champion in three different weight classes and beat all the top Heavyweight Boxers of his time except, Rocky Marciano. However, to his credit, he is the only man ever to finish a 15 round bout standing with the undefeated, Marciano. Ezzard beat Jersey Joe Walcott, Joey Maxim, Archie Moore, and the great Joe Louis. I very much enjoyed watching Ezzard's style and finesse in the ring.

JERSEY JOE WALCOTT

Arnold Raymond Cream
B: January 31, 1914 D: February 25, 1994
Born: Pennsauken, New jersey
6' 0" / 195 lbs.
Record: 51-18-2 32 KO's

Champion:
July 18, 1951 - September 23, 1952

Arnold Raymond Cream was born into the low-income area in Pennsauken, New Jersey, to his father from St. Thomas, Virgin Islands, and mother from Jordantown, New Jersey. Arnold's father died when he was 15 years old, which naturally caused a hardship on the family. Arnold proudly decided to quit school and took employment at a local soup factory to help support his mother, eleven brothers, and sisters.

The new breadwinner also picked up on Boxing at 16 years old in his energetic, spare time. As he got serious about Boxing, Arnold decided that he needed a Boxing "ring name." He chose "Joe Walcott" whose name was his idol and Welterweight Champion "Joe Walcott" from Barbados. He then added "Jersey" from his home state, to become, "Jersey Joe Walcott."

The new Jersey Joe Walcott was a naturally talented Boxer and proved it with an easy first-round KO win in his very first bout on September 9, 1930. His excellent counter punching skills and his powerful left hook gave him many wins that continued until his big break at the World Heavyweight Championship in 1949.

Jersey Joe met Ezzard Charles on Wednesday, June 22, 1949, for the National Boxing Association title that the retired champion, Joe Louis, had left open. Joe lasted 15 rounds but lost on a decision to Charles. Ezzard taking on all challengers, gave Jersey Joe another go at his title in March of 1951, but again, Joe lost on a Decision.

In the meantime, the retired Champion, Joe Louis, returned to the ring and challenged Ezzard Charles on Wednesday, September 27, 1950. Charles out pointed Louis and won on a 15-round Decision that handed Joe only his second loss of his career. This bout solidified

Charles' position and qualified him to become the new bona fide World Heavyweight Boxing Champion.

Champion, Ezzard Charles agreed to a third match with Jersey Joe on Wednesday, July 18, 1951, at Forbes Field in Pittsburgh, Pennsylvania. Joe learned something from their first two bouts and used this knowledge to win by KO in the 7th round in Pittsburgh. The new Heavyweight Champion, Jersey Joe Walcott, became the oldest man to win the world title at age thirty-seven and one-half years old. To return the favor, Walcott gave Charles a rematch for their fourth and last meeting. The result was a controversial win by Jersey Joe with a 15-round Unanimous Decision. If the judges had seen the bout as many spectators had, Ezzard would have been the first-ever to regain the Heavyweight title.

Joe's next title defense was against the undefeated Rocky Marciano on Tuesday, September 23, 1952, in Municipal Stadium in Philadelphia, Pennsylvania. Joe's precise punching dropped Rocky in the first round with a left hook, which was a first in the ring for Rocky. Joe continued to be ahead on points, but Marciano's brawling style was to take what his opponent could dish out and come back for more. Rocky was relentless in this fight as usual, and eventually traded right hook punches with Joe in the 13th round. Rocky's punch landed first and contorted Joe's jaw into one of the most devastating punches of Boxing history. Joe collapsed from this punch to hand off the World

Heavyweight Boxing Championship crown to Rocky Marciano, "The Brockton Bomber."

The always accommodating Rocky Marciano offered Jersey Joe a rematch in Chicago Stadium in Chicago, Illinois, on Friday, May 15, 1953. Rocky was just too much for the 39-year-old, Jersey Joe that night, and KO'd him in the first round. Jersey Joe Walcott decided to retire from Boxing after this bout. However, Joe did referee several bouts and was the third man in the ring for the infamous Muhammad Ali - Sonny Liston 1965 bout, in which Ali KO'd Liston.

Jersey Joe was featured as "The Ring" magazine, 'Fighter of the Year" in 1951, "The Ring" Boxing Hall of Fame in 1969, The World Boxing Hall of Fame in 1983, The International Boxing Hall of Fame 1990, and The New Jersey Hall of Fame in 2013. After retiring, Jersey Joe appeared on some TV shows and acted in a few movies. He also directed special projects for the New Jersey Department of Community Affairs that helped the disabled children. Joe was elected the Sheriff in Camden County, New Jersey, and in 1975 to 1984 was the prestigious Chairman of the New Jersey Athletic Commission.

Jersey Joe Walcott died in 1994 of Diabetes at the age of 80. He was laid to rest in Sunset Memorial Park, Pennsauken, Camden County, New Jersey.

MY OBSERVATION

I've watched the Jersey Joe Walcott bouts against Ezzard Charles and Joe Louis and was very impressed.

Joe had many traits and talents that combined to make the great Boxer that he was. He very much looked like "The Greatest," Muhammad Ali, to me. He had an excellent flipping jab that he could land going forward or backward like Ali. Joe could also quickly stop and deliver a right hand without notice. He, too, had superb, broken rhythm footwork, and was very mobile, making him hard to hit.

Jersey Joe also had those tremendous defensive skills in which he could slip and block most punches. He was a smooth and entertaining Boxer that was a pleasure to watch. Jersey Joe is one of my favorites!

ROCKY MARICANO

"The Brocton Bomber"

B: September 1, 1923 D: August 31, 1969
Born: Brockton Massachusetts
5' 10" / 185lbs.
Record: 49-0 43 KO's

Champion:
September 23, 1952 - April 27, 1956
Retired Undefeated

Rocco Francis Marchegiano was the son of Italian immigrants and one of six siblings. Rocco's start was a rough one as he contracted pneumonia and nearly died when he was very young. However, after this illness, Rocco became quite an athlete who played baseball, football, wrestled, and enjoyed lifting weights in school. He and his friends also liked to punch an old mailbag in his backyard before boxing with each other for fun. However, his first love back then was baseball. With his powerful swing, he could easily knock the ball out of the park.

Things changed when Rocco was on the high school football team and decided to play on his church league team too. This was against the coach's rules, and when he found out that Rocco was playing for the church team, the coach cut him from the school squad. Rocco was so angry that he decided to just quit school altogether after the 10th grade. However, he thought it was just as well because he felt that he could and should work to help support his large family.

Jobs for a young man with no skills gave Rocco a list of hard, undesirable jobs. He ended up with hard labor jobs like ditch digging, a railroad layer, and a dock worker for an ice and coal company. He eventually got another demanding job as a "puller" at the Stacy Adams shoe factory where his father worked. His father objected to the hard labor jobs and their conditions, but he knew Rocco had his mind set on working there. He knew that Rocco didn't mind hard labor and wanted to help the family. His particular job as a "puller" developed tremendous upper body strength, which helped him later in his career as a very powerful puncher. He also gained muscle through the popular Charles Atlas program.

At age 20, Rocco was inducted into the US Army in 1943 during WWll and was sent to England to serve for several months. As the war ended, he was brought back to the states and stationed at Fort Lewis, Washington. While at this army base, he had two choices for duty, kitchen work or Boxing. This was not a hard decision for Rocco because he loved Boxing. He quickly developed into a tough competitor with a winning record. Shortly after the war, he entered the 1946 US Armed Forces Boxing Tournament and won the title.

After being released from the US Army, Rocco didn't pursue Boxing, but drifted back to his first love, baseball. Right away he tried out for the Chicago Cubs baseball team proving his great hitting talents. However, he wasn't a complete player. Rocky couldn't throw well enough to make the club.

Rocky returned home and with baseball out of the picture, he decided Boxing was the alternative that he would like to pursue. He felt that he could possibly become successful and earn a living with his second choice.

After some amateur bouts, Rocco turned pro on a Monday, July 12, 1948, meeting Harry Bilazarian. His powerful punching style knocked out this opponent and earned him a win at his very first outing.

As Rocco was introduced to the audiences in his early career, the ring announcers had problems pronouncing "Marchegiano," his last name. So, he knew that he had to a make change in his ring name as some Boxers had done before him. Rocco decided "Rocky" should be the first name, and Marchegiano should be shortened to "Marciano." Rocco Marchegiano then became "Rocky Marciano."

As he developed a following, his style became apparent that he was as a brawler, mauler, and slugger. Rocky would lead with his head and could take a punch. It's been said that "he would take ten punches to give one of his." Rocky also had an awkward style with his constant movement and threw punches from so many angles that made it hard to deal with him.

Rocky fought most of his bouts in the northeastern US, primarily in the New England area. Twenty-eight of his forty-nine bouts were at the Rhode Island Auditorium in Providence, Rhode Island. Rocky met the best fighters of the day and some who were just journeymen trying their luck. However, they all went down in defeat. Ezzard Charles, Jersey Joe Walcott, and Joe Louis seemed to be the three Boxers that the Rocky fans seem to remember the most.

On Saturday, October 27, 1951, Rocky took on challenger, former Champion, and his idol, Joe Louis. Joe had retired two years earlier and was on the comeback trail to earn very needed funds and regain the Heavyweight title if possible. Rocky was much younger, but was the underdog leading up to the bout.

From the beginning, it was evident that the ex-Champ, Louis, was not the fighter as before. Joe didn't give Rocky the opposition that he would have in previous years, as he had lost much of his sharpness. Rocky could also tell that Joe wasn't the challenge of old and didn't want to demoralize his idol, but decided it was better to end the punishment with an 8th round KO. The crowd booed Rocky as the iconic, national hero, Joe Louis went down in defeat. The fall of his idol also greatly saddened Rocky. It's known that Rocky even shed a tear for Joe in his dressing room after the fight. Rocky said that he thought that it had been a bad idea for Joe to return to the ring, but understood that he did it because of his financial woes. This was the last fight for the great Champion, Joe Louis. Rocky saw this sad and undesirable situation and remembered this lesson when he later retired himself.

On Tuesday, September 23, 1952, Rocky challenged the current Champion, Jersey Joe Walcott, in Philadelphia for the title. Walcott dropped Rocky in the very first round and was outboxing him until the 13th round. Rocky's relentless style then paid off. In this round, both men threw devastating right hooks at the same, in which Rocky's landed first. Rocky's right hook punch had a slight overhand angle, which he called his "Susie Q." The punch landed onto Walcott's jaw to knock him out with one of the most iconic Boxing snapshots of all time. This day, Rocky became the new World Heavyweight Boxing Champion with this face shattering KO punch of Jersey Joe Walcott.

A year later, Rocky granted the 37-year-old Jersey Joe a rematch on Friday, May 15, 1953. Walcott just couldn't move and box in this fight as before. Rocky KO'd Walcott in the very first round to go home early. Next, Roland LaStarza challenged Rocky and was holding his own until the Champ caught LaStarza and KO'd him in the 11th round for his second title defense.

The next title defense for Rocky was ex-champ and 33-year-old Ezzard Charles on Thursday, June 17, 1954. Ezzard boxed Rocky to survive, but lost a 15-round decision. Incidentally, with this match, Charles became the only man to last 15 rounds with Rocky. The very next year the Champ gave Charles another rematch on Friday, September 17, 1954. Like ex-champ Jersey Joe Walcott, Ezzard Charles succumbed to a KO, but in the 8th round. Next, Rocky gave European Champion, Don Cockrell a shot at the world title on Monday, May 16, 1955. Cockrell just didn't have the opposition and went down in the 9th round.

Rocky had one more title defense and his last bout. It was on Wednesday, September 21, 1955, against former Light Heavyweight Champion and Boxing sensation, Archie Moore. Moore is also considered one of the best Light Heavyweight Champions in Boxing history. Like Walcott and Charles, the 38-year-old Archie Moore began to outbox Rocky early and did drop him in the 2nd round. However, Rocky's relentless style wore down the older challenger and added another KO to his record in the 9th round. This gave Rocky his undefeated, 49-0 record with a knockout percentage at 87%. He is also the only undefeated Heavyweight Champion in Boxing history with a no losses or draws. Some former Champions retired undefeated, but returned to the ring and sustained some losses to undo their perfect record.

The closest to Rocky's record is Larry Holmes, with a 48-0 record. Larry met Michael Spinks on Saturday, September 21, 1985, in Las Vegas. In sight of Rocky's record. Larry lost a very controversial Decision in a production of promoters, Don King and Butch Lewis. It was no secret that King and Holmes were not friends. Holmes signed to meet Spinks again, but also lost the rematch on Saturday, April 19, 1986, in which was even more controversial.

Rocky retired undefeated on Friday, April 27, 1956, at age 31. He was offered a million dollars to return to the ring, but he remembered the men that tried to come back before him, including his idol, Joe Louis. Unlike many other Champions who returned to earn money, Rocky was financially stable. It's reported that his net worth was a million dollars, (which would be $9,426,066.18 today). In retirement, however, Rocky did re-enter the ring as a Boxing referee, a Wrestling referee, ringside commentator, and made some TV appearances. He also became a partner in some Italian restaurants.

As Muhammad Ali emerged onto the scene as "The Greatest," the question in many minds was, who was the greatest, Rocky or Ali? So, to calculate the answer to this interesting question, movie producers,

Boxing historians, Rocky, and Ali all came together to determine the potential outcome. One series of calculations gave Rocky the win, and another gave Ali the victory. This documentary aired on TV on Tuesday, January 20, 1970. Sadly, Rocky never saw it air due to the small plane crash that killed him one day before his 46th birthday on Sunday, August 31, 1969, near Des Moines, Iowa. A night flight in bad weather and possible pilot error seems to be the causes of the crash. The Boxing world was shocked and saddened to lose their undefeated American Boxing icon.

Rocky was inducted into the National Italian American Sports of Fame in 1977 and the International Boxing Hall of Fame in 1990. The World Boxing Council erected a bronze statue of Rocky in his hometown of Brockton, Massachusetts. As a tribute to his father, another statue of Rocky was erected in his father's hometown of Teatina, Italy.

Many documentaries and movies were made in reference to Rocky, including some inspiration of Sylvester Stallone in his "Rocky" movies. Rocky is considered by many Boxing historians and experts as one of the greatest Heavyweight Champions of all time. He is always ranked in the top ten in all Boxing surveys and polls.

Rocky Marciano's perfect record still stands, as he is the only undefeated World Heavyweight Boxing Champion with a no losses or draws. He was laid to rest in a crypt in Forest Lawn Cemetery in Fort Lauderdale, Florida.

MY OBSERVATION

Rocky Marciano's style was more like plowing through a field rather than a boxing in the ring. He plowed through his opponents, keeping them off balance and jamming their punches. This approach would eventually wear his opponents down in order for him to finish them off.

Rocky's style would be classified as a "Brawler," "Mauler," or sometimes a "Swarmer." He used primarily hook punches, uppercuts, and overhand punches, including his favorite, his right overhand, in which he called his "Susie Q." He would also take several punches from the "Boxers" to land just one of his.

"The Rock" had tremendous upper body strength, which made just one of his punches devastating. However, you could see him throw his punches so hard and wildly, that he would sometimes nearly throw himself down.

Rocky, the "Brawler' and current Champion, did meet the ex-Champion, Joe Louis, the "Boxer," in 1951. This type of matchup is commonly called "The Battle of the Styles" (incidentally, another high-profile type matchup like this was Ali and Joe Frazier in the 1970s). Rocky did KO Joe in the 8th round, but Joe was well past his prime. I would like to have seen the outcome if they both were in their prime at the same time. I believe that Rocky Marciano and Joe Louis were each the very best of their respective styles. Rocky is the first

Boxer that I remember as a kid. My dad and I used to watch the professionals on a national TV production of Boxing called "Gillette's Friday Night Fights". We also watched Saturday's "Tomorrow's Champions," which was hosted by Ed Callay on WAVE-TV in Louisville in the 1950s.

Rocky's style and approach did work for him as he is the only undefeated Heavyweight Champion in Boxing history with no losses or draws.

FLOYD PATTERSON

B: January 4, 1935 D: May 11, 2006
Born: Waco, North Carolina
6'0" / 185 lbs.
Record: 55-8-1 40 KO's

Champion:
November 30, 1956 - June 26, 1959
June 20, 1960 - September 25, 1962

Floyd Patterson was one of ten children who was born in Waco, North Carolina, but moved to Brooklyn, New York when he was ten years old. The family was impoverished, and his father took on hard labor jobs to support them. He worked construction, as a longshoreman, and at the sanitation department.

Floyd was a mild-mannered kid that seemed to have an introverted personality. He had his problems as a kid, didn't like going to school, and avoided showing up most days. The officials decided to send Floyd to a reform school in New York to help turn him around. This was near the Gramercy Gym, where his brothers were already working out with the local Boxing trainer, Cus D'Amato. At fourteen years old, Floyd decided to try Boxing with Cus and his brothers, who roughed him up on a regular basis. Cus could see Floyd's potential and was willing to give him some special attention. Cus also became a good influence on Floyd's disposition and attitude through Boxing as he had on many other boys that needed direction. Incidentally, Cus D'Amato was also the trainer and responsible for "Iron" Mike Tyson and in his success.

Floyd quickly developed and won the AAU tournament in the Welterweight division in January of 1950. He also won the Middleweight division in Chicago in 1951. Floyd had only one loss in his first several amateur bouts. He developed a unique "Peek a Boo" defense and a very successful leaping aggressive style. He also used a low, crouched position and had very quick punches that could hit an opponent many times before they could barely react.

Floyd's constant training paid off as he won the 1952 New York Golden Gloves Middleweight Championship and the National Amateur Middleweight title. Floyd also won the Olympic Gold Medal in the Middleweight division in Helsinki, Finland, at 19 years old in 1952. Floyd's amateur record grew to 40 wins and only four losses with 31 knockouts. He lost one controversial bout to World Light Heavyweight Champion, Joey Maxim, on Saturday, June 19, 1954.

Floyd eventually moved up to the Light Heavyweight division and became the winningest and considered one of the best Light Heavyweights of all time. He continued in this division until 1956 when Rocky Marciano retired and left the Heavyweight title spot vacant. There was a six-man box off tournament held to determine the next World Champion. Floyd's first match was with a very talented Tommy "Hurricane" Jackson. It was a hard-fought match, but Floyd did win this bout by a Split Decision.

His next match was against another Light Heavyweight sensation and former Champion, Archie Moore. On Friday, November 30, 1956, in Chicago, Illinois, Floyd walked through Moore, knocking him out in the 5th round with his consistent left hooks. This win declared Floyd Patterson the youngest man, at 21 years old, to win the Heavyweight Boxing Championship of the World! Incidentally, Muhammad Ali had just turned 22 years old, and Mike Tyson was 20 years and four months when they won their Championship Crown. This win also made Floyd the first Olympic Gold medalist to become the

World Heavyweight Champion. Floyd only lost one controversial bout in his first thirty-five bouts.

The new Champion had four title defenses before meeting Ingemar Johansson of Sweden at the Polo Grounds in New York on Friday, June 26, 1959. Patterson never got into the bout as he was floored seven times in the 3rd round. Ingemar's favorite punch, the right cross, kept connecting to shock and stop Floyd in that third round. This night, Ingemar Johansson became the new Lineal Heavyweight Champion of the World.

Johansson gave Floyd a rematch at the same site, the Polo Grounds, on Wednesday, June 20, 1960. Floyd was prepared for anything this time as he returned to the ring against the man that took his crown. He was well aware of Johansson's right cross this time, which made this a different fight indeed. Floyd's famous left hook punches were on target this time as he knocked out Johansson in the 5th round to regain his title. This event permitted Floyd to become the first Heavyweight in history to regain the title. Jack Dempsey, Joe Louis, Ezzard Charles, Jersey Joe Walcott, Ingemar Johansson, Sonny Liston, and others have tried and failed.

Floyd returned the favor and offered Johansson their third bout, a "rubber match," on Friday, March 13, 1961, in Miami Beach, Florida. This bout started with both fighters trading punches as Johansson knocked Floyd down twice in the 6th round. Like a true Champion, Floyd rose, fought on, and knocked out Johansson at the end of the sixth round.

After two defenses, Floyd took a challenge from bigger and stronger, Sonny Liston. Liston was a feared opponent who was commonly called "The Bear." Floyd's trainer, Cus D'Amato, wanted Floyd to avoid the heavier opponents for as long as possible and begged him not to take the Liston bout, but Floyd ignored his mentor. They had a major disagreement in which Cus was disgusted and walked out on Floyd.

Floyd agreed to the bout at Comiskey Park in Chicago, Illinois, on September 25, 1962. Cus was right; Sonny Liston was just too much for the smaller, Floyd Patterson. Floyd punched, slipped, and was holding his own until Liston caught Floyd. Liston only took two minutes and six seconds of the first round to KO the Champ. Sonny Liston, without much of a fight, became the new World Heavyweight Boxing Champion.

Sonny gave Floyd a title rematch at the Las Vegas Convention the next year on Sunday, July 22, 1963. The story was the same, another first-round knockout. However, Floyd didn't give up; he went back to the gym to regroup.

Floyd was next paired with another taller and larger opponent, the current Champion, Muhammad Ali. Ali seemed to be too big and was seven years younger. Ali dominated the bout and won with a TKO in the 12th round on Monday, November 22, 1965, in Las Vegas.

Three years later, Floyd got another shot at the title

against another taller, bigger, and current champion, Jimmy Ellis also from Louisville, Kentucky. This bout was at Rasunda Stadium in Stockholm, Sweden, on Saturday, September 14, 1968. Incidentally, Ellis was Ali's childhood friend, training and sparring partner, amateur, and professional opponent. Ellis had won a "box off" tournament to determine who would become the next World Heavyweight Champion when Ali lost the title in 1967.

Floyd faced Jimmy as his first title defense at 33 years old. Floyd fought like a true champion, but the bigger Jimmy's Ellis was able to knock Floyd down and win on a close Decision to retain the crown.

Floyd decided to fight one more time in a rematch against with now former Champ, Muhammad Ali. They met in Madison Square Garden, New York, on Wednesday, September 20, 1972, for the North American Boxing Federation title. Ali dominated the bout until the fight had to be stopped due to a cut of Floyd's eye in the 7th round, which was a TKO win for Ali. Floyd was 37 years old, and he felt that it was the right age to retire. He had a great record and was really a Light Heavyweight who really did well with opponents nearer his size.

Floyd continued his love of Boxing as he trained and managed his adopted son to the WBC World Super Bantamweight title. They were the first father and son to win world Boxing titles. Floyd also opened his own gym in New Platz, New York, after he retired. He trained the underprivileged and troubled kids that would come his way. He also trained Champion Donovan Razor Ruddock in 1992. Ruddock was once matched against former WBA Champion also from Louisville, Greg Page, (Greg trained at my gym for many years), Phil Jackson, and England's Lennox Lewis.

Floyd was named "Rookie of the Year" in New York in 1953, inducted into the "U.S. Olympic Hall of Fame" in 1987, and "The International Boxing Hall of Fame" in 1991. He served two terms as the Chairman of the New York State Athletic Commission beginning in 1995.

During this time, Floyd began to suffer from Alzheimer's disease, then developed prostate cancer. Floyd Patterson died on Thursday, May 11, 2006, at the age of 71 and was laid to rest at New Platz Rural Cemetery, New Platz, New York.

MY OBSERVATION

Floyd Patterson was not interested in school and learning when he was a youngster. He decided that he wasn't going to attend regular school, which landed him in reform school. This oddly worked out for him since he met the man who turned his life around through Boxing. The compassionate Cus D'Amato helped many kids that needed direction and motivation.

Floyd became one of Cus' many students as did another such kid 30 years later, Mike Tyson. In my last 50 years in my gym, I've also had many kids that needed extra attention and guidance.

Very often, a person doesn't conform to the conventional system of education as they seem to be more artistic such as musicians, painters, sculptors, writers, and of course, Martial Artists. Floyd belonged to this group. Floyd did become successful and Champion through the art of Boxing at just age 21. However, most of the heavyweights now were over 200 pounds. Floyd eventually faced the larger challengers like Sonny Liston, Muhammad Ali, and Jimmy Ellis. These men were 30 pounds heavier and about 4 inches taller. His quick hands and leaping left hook just couldn't match their size. Bigger men can jam or block this style and the lighter weight of the smaller man. That's why there are weight divisions of about seven pounds or so below the heavyweight division. I remember the excitement of Floyd Patterson when I was a kid in the 1950s.

INGEMAR JOHANSSON

"Ingo"

B. Sept. 22, 1932 D. Jan. 30, 2009
Born: Gothenburg, Sweden
6' 1" / 195 lbs.
Record: 26-2 17 KO's

Champion:
June 26, 1959 - June 20, 1960

Ingemar Johansson was the third European
Champion to win the World Heavyweight Boxing

Championship after Max Schmeling of Germany in 1930 and Primo Carnera of Italy in 1933, under the use of the Marquess of Queensbury rules.

Ingemar was a handsome, easy living, Swede that had one exceptional Boxing tool, a "cannon-like" right hand. He referred to his right cross as "Toonder" of his "Toonder and Lighting."

Ingemar began Boxing at 13 years old and was so successful that he became a member of the European Golden Gloves team in 1951 at 19 years old. He was also on the team that fought in the Olympic Games in Helsinki in 1952. He ended his amateur career with a 60-11 record and 31 KO's before turning pro in 1952.

Ingemar had five Championship bouts outside Sweden, one in Denmark, one in Italy, and three with Floyd Patterson in New York. He had one win in Germany, but conveniently for him, all other bouts in his career were in Sweden. As a pro, his wins compiled, and with just his fourth bout, won the Scandinavian Heavyweight title in 1953 against Erik Jensen in Denmark. He also won the European Heavyweight title on September 30, 1956, against Franco Cavicchi in Bologna, Italy, as his fifteenth bout. He maintained his European titles until challenging the World Heavyweight Champion, Floyd Patterson, from the United States. Ingemar didn't mind that he was the 5 to 1 underdog when they met at Yankee Stadium in New York on June 26, 1959.

Ingemar stayed away from Patterson and boxed for two rounds until, out of nowhere, his cannon like right cross caught Patterson like "toonder". Patterson went down like a rock and never regained his senses. Ingemar dropped the Champion six more times until the referee called a halt to the bout. This surprise gave "Ingo" a TKO win in just the 3rd round. Boxing fans couldn't believe that this relatively unknown from far away Sweden was now the new Undisputed World Heavyweight Boxing Champion.

Ingermar Johansson was the first Swede to own this title. Of course, Patterson was awarded a rematch that took place a year later on June 20, 1960, at the Polo Grounds in New York. Patterson was much more careful this time as he stayed away from Ingermar's deadly right hand. Patterson returned the favor as he executed his favorite punch, a leaping left hook. Patterson landed this explosive punch perfectly in the fifth round that knocked Ingemar cold. He was asleep before he hit the canvas. The blow was so devastating that it knocked Ingemar out for five minutes and groggy for several more minutes. This win made Floyd Patterson the first man to ever recapture the Undisputed World Heavyweight title.

Floyd Patterson made good on his promise once again and met Ingemar for a third bout. It took place nine months later at Miami Beach, Florida, on March 13, 1961. "Ingo" came in out of shape, but performed surprisingly well to drop Patterson twice early in the contest. However, Patterson also floored Ingermar twice and with his poor conditioning, had little chance left. The referee stopped the bout in the 6th round after

Ingemar hit the canvas once more, and Patterson retained his world title.

Ingemar returned to Sweden for four more bouts, including a match against Dick Richardson for the European Heavyweight title on June 17, 1962. He KO'd Richardson in the 8th round to recapture his old title. At age 30, Ingemar fought his last match against Brian London on April 21, 1963, in Stockholm, Sweden. He displayed a lackluster performance, but was leading on points; then, the Champ was dropped and nearly experienced a KO in the 12th and final round. Luckily, Ingemar was saved by the bell in the last few seconds. Ingo decided then that it was time to "throw in the towel" and retire. Actually, seven years later, at age 37, he contemplated returning to the ring, but couldn't get into shape and wisely stayed in retirement.

During retirement, Ingemar stayed very busy as a Boxing commentator, promoter, appeared on TV, several movies, had a hit record, and wrote an autobiography titled, "Seconds Out of The Ring." He also became a businessman with a fishing boat, a bar, and a hotel in Pompano Beach, Florida.

Ingemar graced the cover of "Sports Illustrated" and "Life" magazines and was named the "Male Athlete of The Year" in 1959. He was also named the Third Best Swedish athlete in the 20th century by The Swedish Sports Academy. He was inducted into The World Boxing Hall of Fame in 1988, The International Hall of Fame in 2002, and a bronze statue of him was erected in his hometown of Gothenburg, Sweden, in 2011.

Ingemar was struck with Alzheimer's disease and Dementia around 1999. He suffered from these illnesses until he died of pneumonia on January 30, 2009, at the age of 76. His funeral was at Yasa Church in his hometown of Gothenburg, Sweden. He was buried in the Vastra Kyrkogarden Cemetery, Goteborg, Goteborgs Kommun, Vastra Gotalands Ian, Sweden.

MY OBSERVATION

Ingemar could have been known as a Hollywood movie star or Playboy jet setter. He was a handsome man who liked to box some and play some. His primary role will be remembered as the underdog who upset the World Champion, Floyd Patterson in 1959. After he retired, he did so many things, including TV, movies, singing, writing, and more. Ingemar was a multi-talented person who added a little pizazz to Boxing.

CHARLES "SONNY" LISTON

"The Bear"

B. May 8, 1932 D. Dec. 30,1970
Born: San Slough, Arkansas
6' 1" / 219 lbs.
Record 50-4 39 KO's

Champion:
Sept. 25, 1962 - Feb. 25, 1964

C harles "Sonny" Liston was born into a large sharecropping family in Johnson Township,

Arkansas. His birthdate was somewhere between 1930 and 1932; he didn't know for sure. His farming family was not highly educated, and he didn't get many days in school himself. His father had 25 children who worked on their family farm, and it's been written that his father was abusive to the children, including Charles. One day, Charles' mother had finally had enough of her life in Arkansas and moved to St. Louis, MO. She took some of the siblings with her, but not Charles. To avoid his father's abusiveness, Charles found the money and joined his mother in St. Louis when he was just 13 years old.

Charles enrolled in school there, but with little education and naturally low self-esteem, he had to be placed in the first grade. The other kids in the school taunted and teased him about his lack of education and size, which definitely lowered his confidence even further. To avoid more ridicule and scorn, Charles decided not to return for the second grade.

Without school to keep Charles busy and learning, he easily drifted toward the wrong crowd and began robbing and looting for his past time. Naturally, after some time, he was caught and sentenced to five years at the Missouri State Penitentiary on Thursday, June 1st, 1950. He was just 18 years old. Luckily, the Athletic Director at the prison took an interest in Charles and suggested that he channel his energy and time into Boxing. This was a great outlet for Charles viewing his past troubled childhood. Charles took the official's advice and dedicated himself to the program for the next two and a half years. Then, his good behavior and hard work got him early parole. He left prison on October 31st, 1952.

Charles continued Boxing and began a winning career as he captured a Golden Gloves title and the Intercity Title in Chicago in March 1953. He also won the International Golden Gloves in St. Louis on June 23rd, 1953, over German, Herman Schreibner.

Charles turned pro in September 1953 and met his first opponent, Don Smith, on September 2, 1953. Smith was a demeaning kind of guy who called Charles "Sonny" continually before the fight, and oddly this nickname stuck. It seems that Don Smith was better at talking than boxing, as "Sonny" creamed him 33 seconds into the first round.

Sonny sailed through the first seven opponents until he had an off night and lost a Split Decision against Marty Marshall on September 7, 1954. However, he avenged his loss in two rematches against Marshall, once in 1955 and once in 1956.

Due to Sonny's criminal record and connections, he was monitored very closely by law enforcement. In an altercation on May 5, 1956, an officer confronted him in which Sonny fought back with the officer, breaking his knee, smashing his face, and taking his gun. This incident got Sonny jailed again and was banned from Boxing until 1958. When he was released, he moved to Philadelphia and took on a job in construction with a new manager who was said to be connected to the

"Underworld". Many sources believe that Sonny stayed connected to the Underworld until his death.

Sonny won eight bouts in 1958 and four more in 1959, including one against Cleveland Williams, a very formidable heavyweight, in just three rounds. In 1960, he won five more bouts against top contenders and therefore was declared the number one contender to the Heavyweight Championship throne. However, many individuals and groups didn't want Sonny to be the Heavyweight Champion because of his past behavior and alleged ties to the "Underworld." It's recorded that President John F. Kennedy, in a visit from Champion Floyd Patterson, asked him not to offer a title shot to Sonny. Cus D'Amato, Floyd Patterson's trainer, also begged Floyd to avoid Sonny, for several reasons, with no luck. Taking no one's advice, Patterson gave Sonny a title shot on Tuesday, September 25, 1962, in Comiskey Park in Chicago, Illinois. D'Amato, future Champion Cassius Clay, and 8-5 betting odds all favored Liston to win. However, most reporters and most former Champions thought Floyd was too fast and mobile for Liston.

D'Amato, Clay, and the betting world were correct in their assumptions, as Sonny mugged and battered Patterson to a 2:06, first-round knockout. Sonny's twenty-five-pound weight advantage and his crushing hook punches were just too much for the Champion, Floyd Patterson. This was the third-fastest finish in a World Heavyweight title fight, and the first-time a defending Champion was knocked out in the first round. Although Sonny was the new Champion, he was not welcomed back by his hometown of Philadelphia. Actually, Sonny was one of the most disliked Heavyweight Champions in Boxing history. So, Sonny decided to find another hometown, Denver, Colorado.

To be fair, there is a usual rematch clause in the contract for Heavyweight title bouts. Therefore, Sonny and Patterson met for their rematch on Monday, July 22, 1963, in Las Vegas, Nevada. This time, most agreed that Patterson was a 4 to 1 underdog. The odds were correct, as this bout was a rerun of the first meeting as Sonny knocked Patterson down three times in the first round. Sonny stopped the former Champ just four seconds later than their first fight at 2:10 with a barrage of punches. No more meetings between these two were ever scheduled.

Eight months later, Liston offered a young, 1960 Olympic Medal winner, Cassius Clay, a shot at his title. Sonny was a 7 to 1 favorite with nearly all sports writers betting on him. They met for a showdown on Tuesday, February 25, 1964, at Convention Hall in Miami Beach, Florida.

Sonny chased and wildly swung at Clay, who moved and slipped his punches throughout the entire fight. Clay's tactic could have been to see his opponent's choice of combinations, determining the opponent's timing, or just wear Sonny down. As the fight continued, Clay moved, slipped, and stopped with his own combinations. The challenger surprised Sonny with his speed and accuracy as Clay's 1-2 combo caused a cut under Sonny's left eye and bruised him under his right eye. These cuts and bruises required some attention in Sonny's corner between rounds.

Clay's vision oddly became impaired by a burning sensation in the 5th round. Sonny's corner was suspected of intentionally transmitting a substance to impair Clay's vision. In Sonny's defense, attention given to his swelling eye could have been unintentionally transferred from Sonny's gloves upon contact with Clay. We really don't know for sure.

After some slipping and dodging, Clay's eyesight seemed to improve in the 6th round as he began throwing combinations that landed heavily. Clay seemed to be on the path of some payback. Sonny seemed to be hurt, overwhelmed, and surprisingly wouldn't come out for the 7th round. Sonny claimed his shoulder was causing him great pain. His cornermen also agreed that he was hurt in which later medical reports verified that there were some shoulder concerns. However, many Boxing fans said that they believed it was more of an excuse to quit. Regardless, Cassius Clay was the new Lineal World Heavyweight Boxing Champion. The Boxing world was shocked!

Sonny and Clay, now (Muhammad Ali), after some scheduling complications, met for a rematch at the Central Maine Youth Center in Lewiston, Maine, on Tuesday, May 25, 1965. The bout was refereed by former Heavyweight Champ, Jersey Joe Walcott. Midway through the first round, after some punches had landed, Ali threw an arching right cross to counter Sonny's jab, that dropped Sonny like a rock. The right hand didn't look that devastating, but Sonny seemed to be out. There was much confusion on the amount of time given to Sonny to get up off the canvas. The timekeeper started the count right away, but referee Walcott did not, because Ali wouldn't retreat to the neutral corner. Sonny eventually rose to continue the bout, but officials called a halt to the fight awarding Ali the win by TKO. Actually, Liston went down at 1:44, got up at 1:56, and Walcott stopped the bout via the officials at 2:12 of the first round. The punch was quickly coined, "The Phantom Punch." Some said it was a great punch, and others said a punch like that could not take a man down like Sonny Liston. Former Champions and experts agreed that punch may have knocked him down, but not out. Many believe it was a "fix" or "dive" by Sonny. The confusion of the count was similar to "The Long Count" fiasco in September 1927 rematch bout between Jack Dempsey and Gene Tunney. Dempsey would not retreat to his corner after he knocked Tunney down, which gave Tunney extra time to recover. Dempsey possibly didn't regain his title in this rematch by not following this one rule that night.

After Sonny lost to Muhammad Ali, Sonny won by knockout, 13 of his next 14 bouts. He lost only one contest and won his very last fight over contender, Chuck Wepner. Sonny annihilated Wepner as he broke his nose, cheekbone, and gave him 72 stitches to his head.

Sonny was slated to face Canadian George Chuvalo on December 1970, but was suspiciously found dead in his home in Las Vegas beforehand. His death certificate is said to be a heroin overdose causing lung congestion and heart failure. The circumstances about his death were never determined exactly, and the truth was never concluded. Some say Sonny used heroin; some say that he absolutely never would, others say he was murdered by criminal thugs or the Underworld.

Charles "Sonny" Liston's certified day of death is December 30, 1970, at 38 years old. He was laid to rest in Paradise Memorial Gardens in Las Vegas, Nevada.

MY OBSERVATION

Sonny Liston was one of the hardest punchers and most feared Boxers of his time. He was unusually strong with those very explosive punches. Opponents knew that he could end their night quickly with just one punch. Sadly, he was mistreated as a child, which molded his life in a negative way. Consequently, he didn't have a formal education, which no doubt caused him to drift toward crime and people who didn't have his best interest in mind. However, he should be remembered as a good Boxer who catapulted Cassius Clay, (Muhammad Ali) into the superstardom.

MUHAMMAD ALI

"The Greatest"

B. Jan. 17, 1942 D. June 3, 2016
Born: Louisville, Kentucky
6' 3" / 215 lbs.
Record 56-5 37 KO's

Champion:
Feb. 25, 1964 - Ret. 1967
Jan. 28, 1974 - Feb. 15, 1978
Aug. 15, 1978 - Ret. 1979

C assius Marcellus Clay Jr. was one of five sons, and one daughter to Odessa Grady Clay and Cassius Marcellus Clay Senior. Marcellus Clay Sr. was named in honor of 19th Century Cassius Marcellus Clay, a Kentucky lawyer, politician, and three-time Kentucky House member. Nineteenth Century Clay was also a Major General in the Union Army during the Civil War. Clay inherited the family farm when his father died, he immediately freed all slaves of the farm. He then hired them to work for him for quality pay. Clay was a staunch Abolitionist who crusaded for all people to be free. In addition to all his other accomplishments, Clay was appointed as the Ambassador to Russia by President Abraham Lincoln on March 28, 1861. Clay said he would only serve if President Lincoln promised to maintain the quest for freedom for all. Clay was beloved by the Russians and won much support for America. Actually, "Ambassador" Cassius Marcellus Clay is responsible for influencing Russia to sell the territory of Alaska to the United States on March 30, 1867, for 7.2 million dollars.

Cassius Marcellus Clay Sr. of the 1940s provided a good living for his family in the West End of Louisville, Kentucky, as a painter. However, this story begins for Cassius Jr. one day in 1954 when he was riding his bicycle in downtown Louisville. He parked his bike, entered a building for a while, and when he came out, his bike had been stolen. Young Cassius began to look for the thief to take matters into his own hands. As fate would have it, he connected with a policeman by the name of Joe Martin instead. Martin explained to young Cassius that he would need skills in order to handle bad people in situations like this. Consequently, Martin took Cassius into his Boxing club that he operated through a city endorsed program in downtown Louisville. Martin saw natural talent in Cassius as he joined the other Boxers. The older Boxers gave attention to the younger ones for guidance, including Billy Martin and Fred Stoner at the club. Cassius later remarked that Stoner helped him develop his style, which happened to be very similar to the World Middleweight Champion, Sugar Ray Robinson.

Handsome, charismatic, and multi-talented Cassius molded his skills and techniques, as he won his first bout in 1954. Ultimately, his amateur record was a winning 100-5 tally, including six Kentucky Golden Glove titles, two National Golden Glove titles, and one AAU National title. He also won the Light Heavyweight Olympic Gold Medal in Rome, Italy in 1960 while just 18 years old.

Cassius Clay Jr. began the "The Golden Age of Boxing" when he made his pro debut on Saturday, October 29, 1960, with a win over Tunney Hunsaker in a six-rounder in Louisville, Kentucky. He continued winning as he briefly moved on to the camp of former Light Heavyweight Champion, Archie Moore. He didn't stay long because he didn't like the camp's rules and regulations. Since his style was very similar to the great Middleweight Champion, Sugar Ray Robinson, Cassius thought about joining up with

Robinson's camp to train. However, this connection just never materialized. After some consideration and negotiations in 1960, Cassius did partner with a man that he had met earlier in his career, seasoned trainer, Angelo Dundee. Dundee had been training Boxers with his brother at their 5th Street Gym in Miami, Florida.

It was a good partnership as Cassius cruised through his next eighteen bouts before competing in his only bout in 1964 on Tuesday, February 25. Cassius got his title shot, but was a 7-1 underdog to Champion, Sonny Liston. The contest took place at the Miami Beach Auditorium in Miami Beach, Florida.

Cassius Clay later admitted that he was nervous about the upcoming bout with Sonny Liston. He concealed it by taunting, boasting, and belittling Liston in the media, at the weigh-in, and on fight night. This gimmick was also a self-promoting, publicity stunt that he had learned from Wrestler, "Gorgeous George" Wagner. Wagner traveled the Wrestling circuit, taunting, antagonizing, and irritating his opponents and fans at his shows to sell tickets. Clay saw this gimmick pack in at auditoriums, including the Louisville Armory in his hometown. The spectators came to see Gorgeous George get whipped and taught a bit of humility. This spectacle did work and was an effective way to generate ticket sales. So, Cassius staged similar performances and used them to affect his opponents, bring in more spectators, and possibly disguise his apprehension.

Cassius Clay faced the mighty and menacing Sonny Liston for the title with a very defensive approach. As expected, Liston chased the challenger to finish him early. However, only frustration prevailed as Clay's constant movement and flashy combinations seemed to be the answer to Liston's aggressive assault.

This very entertaining matchup had a little bit of everything, including controversy over a stinging chemical that ended up in Cassius' eyes believed to come from Liston's gloves. Cassius survived the 5th round adversity and began his own barrage of combinations that seemed to mentally break Liston. After some damage to Liston's face and a complaint of a pulled shoulder, Liston wouldn't come out for the 7th round. Therefore, Cassius Marcellus Clay became the new Lineal Heavyweight Champion of the World at just 22 years old. Shortly after this title win, Cassius Clay changed his name and became "Muhammad Ali" of the Islam religion.

"Muhammad Ali" gave Sonny Liston a rematch in May 1965 that was scheduled to be in Boston, Massachusetts; however, it was moved to Lewiston, Maine, due to scheduling complications. Liston came out aggressively, but missed with a left hook that left him open to Ali's lighting right cross counterpunch... Ali dropped Liston in the very first round. This controversial punch that ended this fight became known as "The Phantom Punch." This victory solidified Ali's World Heavyweight Crown.

Ali's second opponent of this year was none other

than former World Champion, Floyd Patterson. Ali controlled the match with Patterson as he picked up another TKO win on Monday, 22, 1965, in Las Vegas, Nevada. In 1966, Ali took on five opponents, including George Chuvalo in Toronto, Henry Cooper, and Brian London, both in London, England, disposing of all of them to maintain his perfect record. On November 14, 1966, Ali took on veteran Cleveland Williams and stopped him in the third round with a KO. Ernie Terrell fell next by a Unanimous 15 round defeat on February 6, 1967, in Houston, Texas. Ali had one more matchup against Zora Foley, whom he KO'd in the 7th round on March 22, 1967, in New York to add to his perfect professional record.

In 1967, Ali was summoned to the Selective Service Board for induction into the US Army during the controversial Vietnam War. He refused as a "Conscientious Objector" due to his Muslim religion. The Board disagreed and explained the typical punishment for refusing induction could be imprisonment and a $10,000 fine. Ali was fined, stripped of his Heavyweight Boxing title, and was not permitted to compete in the ring. However, after three years, his sentence was overturned in 1970 by the US Supreme Court, and in 1971 his Boxing license was restored.

On October 26, 1970, Ali met the very tough, Jerry Quarry in Atlanta, Georgia. He was victorious after just three rounds due to cuts to Quarry's face. The comeback trail continued on Monday, December 7,

1970, as Ali took on South American Champion, Oscar Bonavena, in Madison Square Garden in New York City. Bonavena lost by TKO in the 15th round that maintained Ali's perfect record.

Ali's next bout was hailed "The Fight of the Century" as two undefeated Champions met on Monday, March 8, 1971. Ali took on current World Heavyweight Champion, 'Smokin" Joe Frazier. It was a battle of styles, Ali's flashy boxing skills against Frazier's relentless, brawling style. Ali taunted Frazier as a pre-fight ploy to shake Joe's confidence and promote the gate. However, Frazier was not amused and was very irritated at Ali for his demeaning remarks, even though it was all a gimmick. This bout was a very exciting exchange of punishment in which Ali uniquely displayed his technique of "Rope-A- Dope."

Joe eventually dropped Ali in the 15th round and went on to win the bout by a Unanimous Decision. "Smokin" Joe Frazier handed Ali his first professional defeat. This was also the first of three exciting bouts with Frazier that are said to be some of the best meetings in Boxing history! Ali then took on childhood stablemate Jimmy Ellis with a 12th round TKO, Buster Mathis Decision in 12 rounds, and Jurgen Blin in Zurich, Switzerland, with another KO in round seven.

Ali won all six bouts in 1972 as he got back on the comeback trail. Notable opponents were George Chuvalo in a rematch Decision on May 1, in Vancouver, Canada. A Jerry Quarry KO in the 7th on June 29, in

Las Vegas, and a rematch with Floyd Patterson on September 10 in New York with a 7th round KO.

Ali had four bouts in 1973, beginning with Joe Bugner in Las Vegas with a 12-round Decision on Valentine's Day. Next were two bouts with the all-around athlete, Kenny Norton. Norton gave Ali all he wanted plus a broken jaw in the 11th round to win by Decision. Kenny handed Ali his second professional loss on March 21, in 1973. The Ali-Norton rematch took place on September 10 in Los Angeles, in which Ali won a controversial Decision to give each man a win. Ali rounded out the year against Rudi Lubbers with a Decision win in Jakarta on October 20.

The year of 1974 only saw two matches for Muhammad Ali, but two spectacular events indeed! Ali took on "Smokin" Joe Frazier in a rematch to avenge his very first pro loss. People still talk about this tremendous exchange of pain. Ali ultimately won this gladiator style, 15 round Decision of brutality in New York on Monday, January 28. Ali's only other bout of the year was titled by Ali as "The Rumble In The Jungle" against current Champion, "Big" George Foreman. It took place in the Democratic Republic of the Congo on Wednesday, October 30th. Ali "Shook up the World" when he used his "Rope A Dope" to tire Foreman and KO him in the 8th round. This stunning victory was the event that propelled Muhammad Ali to become the Heavyweight Champion of the World for the second time!

An interesting mismatch win in 1975 over Chuck

Wepner, stimulated actor and writer Sylvester Stallone to create the movie character, "Rocky." This was the first win for Ali that year. Ron Lyle fell next in round 11, in Las Vegas on May 16, and Joe Bugner lost by a Decision in Kuala Lumpur on June 30. The feature contest was the third and last one of the year against Joe Frazier. Ali again taunted Frazier in what he called the "Thrilla In Manilla" in the Philippines. They exchanged extreme punishment for 14 grueling rounds until Frazier couldn't take anymore and wouldn't come out for the 15th round. This bout is also considered one of the most exciting matches in Boxing history on October 1, 1975.

Ali faced four more Boxing opponents in 1976 that included Jean Pierre Coopman in San Juan, Puerto Rico, with a 5th round KO on February 20. Jimmy Young lost by decision in Landover, Maryland on April 30, and Richard Dunn in Munich, Germany. The year's last bout was a rematch against imposing Kenny Norton with a controversial win in New York on September 28. However, before Ali took on Kenny Norton, he stepped outside his element to take on Japanese Wrestler, Antonio Inoki, in what he thought was an exhibition bout. However, Inoki saw it as a true contest with limited rules. It turned out to be a boring spectacle with Ali only throwing only six jabs in the 15-round contest. Inoki laid on his back and continuously kicked Ali's left leg. To close the show, the judges called the exhibition a Draw. Ali was hospitalized when he returned to the US with a bruised and infected leg. Blood clots formed, and there was talk of even amputating his leg, but luckily, it finally healed. Next, Ali again faced one of the fiercest opponents of the day, Kenny Norton. After a very close contest, Ali won again.

1977 was a slower year for Ali as he had two Decision wins, one over Alfredo Evangelista in Landover, Maryland, on May 16, and a Unanimous Decision win over Earnie Shavers in New York on September 29th.

Leon Spinks was the only opponent for Ali in 1978, with back to back matches. The first bout saw Ali losing for the third time in his professional career. This was a loss of the Heavyweight title by a Split Decision on Wednesday, February 15, at the Hilton Hotel in Las Vegas. This 15 round Decision loss was a shock to Ali's fans and followers. However, in their rematch on August 15 in the Superdome in New Orleans, Louisiana, Ali regained the crown. This was an unprecedented third time to regain the Championship title with a 15 round Unanimous Decision. The rematch had 70,000 spectators with the largest financial gate in history. In 1979, Ali retired and only performed exhibition bouts as his career was winding down.

Against better judgement, Ali came out of his short retirement and signed for the "The Last Hurrah." This was a title bout against his old sparring partner, Larry Holmes, at Caesar's Palace in Las Vegas on Thursday, October 2, 1980. Ali was just not the performer of old and his cornerman, Angelo Dundee had to step in to stop the bout at the 11th round. A medical exam after the bout proved the beginning signs of Ali's health deterioration. Nevertheless, the bout was seen by two billion viewers, with Ali earning eight million dollars and Holmes six million.

The knowledge of his medical condition did not stop Ali. He ignored the warnings and consequences and agreed to one last bout. It was against Trevor Berbick in Nassau, The Bahamas, on Friday, December 11, 1981. It was another lackluster performance as Ali lost his last bout in a 10-round Decision while displaying much bravery and mental fortitude. He announced his final retirement after this bout at the age of 39 years old. In 1984, Ali was officially diagnosed with Parkinson's Disease.

Ali was a multi-talented Superstar with many talents. He was a singer with Grammy album nominations, films appearances, a Broadway musical, and wrote two autobiographies.

Ali was on countless magazine covers, including "Sports Illustrated" thirty-eight times, he was the Ring Magazine "Fighter of the Year" five times, and the only Boxer named "Boxer of the Year" six times. He was named "Greatest Athlete of the 20th Century"! Sports Illustrated also named him "Sportsman of the Century," and he was inducted into the International Boxing Hall of Fame in 1990.

Ali was a most sought celebrity figure for countless photographers and painters, including the most famous Leroy Neiman. A hometown street in Louisville, Kentucky, was renamed in his honor, and a unique downtown building was built in his honor named "The Ali Center" in 2005. In 2018 the International Airport in Louisville, Kentucky, changed its name to the "Muhammad Ali International Airport."

Ali also earned a star on the Hollywood Walk of Fame, received the Presidential Citizens Medal, and the Presidential Medal of Freedom in 2005.

Ali, the "most recognized man on the planet," was also a true humanitarian and philanthropist. He traveled the world, helping the underprivileged by giving his time and millions of dollars in aid to those in need!

It's believed that Ali earned about 70 million dollars in his career, and it is reported that in 2006, he sold his name for 50 million dollars. His net worth at death is believed to be between 50 and 80 million dollars.

Ali died of respiratory illness and septic shock in Scottsdale, Arizona, at age 74. It's estimated that his memorial service in Louisville was viewed by one billion people. He was laid to rest in Cave Hill Cemetery in his hometown of Louisville, Kentucky.

MY OBSERVATION

Muhammad Ali proclaimed himself as "The Greatest" early in his career and actually did become very, very great. He also became known as "The most recognized man on the planet".

He was a lighting fast heavyweight who could talk as well as he could box. He actually created a new dimension to Boxing by making it a great show rather than just a competition. Once he achieved fame, he used his notoriety and wealth to help others to have a better life all around the world.

I was also born in Louisville and lived not far from him when we were both young. We all followed his career, and I saw him many times when he came back to town during his visits. It was my privilege to have Ali's long-time friend and the former World Champion Jimmy Ellis at my gym in New Albany, Indiana for many years. I was also proud to have Ali's nephew, Ibn Ali, who became a Cruiserweight Champion, start at our gym.

The world is undoubtedly a better place, thanks to Muhammad Ali!

JIMMY ELLIS

B: Feb. 24, 1940 D. May 6, 2014
Born: Louisville, Ky.
6' 1" / 190 lbs.
Record: 40-12-1 24 KO's

Champion:
April 27, 1968 - Feb.16, 1970

James Albert Ellis was a member of a religious family that included ten children. Jimmy's father was a pastor in Louisville, Kentucky, who saw that they lived a very Christian life. Jimmy also sang in the church choir and later in his own gospel group.

Jimmy was a reserved person who was very gracious to everyone that he met. He never bragged about his talents, career, and or boasted about his Heavyweight Championship title.

Jimmy actually trained at the same Columbia Gym in downtown Louisville that young Cassius Clay (Muhammad Ali) belonged to in the 1950's.

One Saturday afternoon, Jimmy watched a friend compete against Clay on a local Boxing show called "Tomorrow's Champions." Jimmy decided that he would join that Boxing gym because he believed that he could also be a good Boxer. He did join the club and quickly fit right in with his natural talents and very likable personality. Of course, Jimmy sparred with then, Cassius Clay, and even competed against him twice as an amateur. Clay won the first bout, and Jimmy won the second. Jimmy quickly collected 59 wins of 66 amateur fights, including a Golden Gloves title in 1960.

Jimmy turned pro in 1961 and left Joe Martin for manager and trainer, Bud Brunner, also in Louisville. They complied a Middleweight record of 15 wins and 5 losses with 6 KOs. However, Jimmy decided that he would benefit by moving over to Clay's new trainer, Angelo Dundee, in Miami, Florida. Dundee took on Jimmy, letting him spar with others, including Clay, which helped them all. Jimmy also had bouts on Clay's undercard as they were both rising stars. As Jimmy developed into a Light Heavyweight, he was beating opponents that were much heavier than him. Actually, as his career continued, he usually fought opponents that outweighed him by 10 to 30 pounds. However, his expert skills and natural talents made him a champion Boxer regardless of the disadvantage.

Cassius Clay, now Muhammad Ali, lost his title in 1967 as a "Conscientious Objector," which left the throne open to fill. Jimmy was included in an eight-man "box-off" tournament of the top contenders to see who would become the next World Heavyweight Champion. Jimmy first fought Leotis Martin as the underdog on Saturday, August 5, 1967, in Houston, Texas. Jimmy overwhelmed Martin until the referee had seen enough and stopped the bout in the 9th round.

Jimmy was again the underdog against his next opponent, South American Champion, Oscar Bonavena, on Saturday, December 2, 1967, in Jimmy's hometown of Louisville, Kentucky. Jimmy surprised the experts once again as he took charge and ultimately won a 12 round Unanimous Decision for his second of three bouts in the tournament.

Next, Jimmy took on a tough Jerry Quarry on Saturday, April 27, 1968, for the third and final bout and the WBA Heavyweight Championship title. Jimmy fought a strategic bout and won by a Split Decision. With this win, Jimmy became the new World Heavyweight Champion. He followed Muhammad Ali, his lifelong friend, sparring partner from the same gyms, and same hometown, Louisville, Kentucky.

Five months later, Jimmy was back in the ring to defend his title against the former Heavyweight Champion, Floyd Patterson. They met in Stockholm, Sweden, on Saturday, September 14, 1968. Jimmy dropped Patterson several times, but the former Champ fought back ferociously, giving Jimmy a broken nose. However, Jimmy prevailed and was awarded the bout by the referee in a close Decision to retain the title.

Jimmy had several more title defenses lined up, but all seemed to fall apart for one reason or another. After some time, his next title defense did materialize against New York State Heavyweight Champion, Joe Frazier. They met at Madison Square Garden in New York City days before Jimmy's 30th birthday on Monday, February 16, 1970. Frazier was tenacious, and his inside fighting proved to be just too much for Jimmy as Angelo Dundee stopped the match before the 5th round. This win gave Joe Frazier the Lineal World Heavyweight title.

However, Jimmy came right back with three wins, one with a TKO win over Robert Davilla and a KO win over Tony Doyle both in Miami. He added a Unanimous Decision over George Chuvalo in Toronto, Canada.

Jimmy's next big bout was against his childhood friend, sparring partner, and amateur opponent, Muhammad Ali. They met in the Houston Astrodome on July 26, 1971. Things were going well for Jimmy until he hurt his right hand, which gave him a significant disadvantage going forward. Jimmy couldn't perform competitively which caused the referee to stop the bout in the 12ᵗʰ round.

Again, Jimmy was not discouraged; he came back and won his next eight bouts by knockouts all taking place in the US. This string of wins earned him a rematch with the now Champion and past challenger to his title, "Smokin" Joe Frazier. This time the contest took place in Melbourne, Australia, on Saturday, March 2, 1975. Jimmy moved and boxed, but couldn't keep the relentless Joe Frazier away. Ultimately, the match was stopped in the ninth round giving Frazier the TKO win.

Jimmy, once again, was not one to be discouraged. He came right back, taking on Carl Baker in Orlando, Florida, on May 6, 1975. Jimmy handed Baker a first-round KO on his comeback trail. Tragically, Jimmy was thumbed in the left eye during training, which left him unable to compete... this ended his ring career.

Boxing had been a deep passion for Jimmy since childhood. Therefore, his passion and personality made it only natural for him to share his knowledge with others to grow and develop. He was hired by the Louisville Parks Department to run the athletic and recreational projects to help the city's youth. Jimmy also stayed in the Boxing gym, training others to promote their career. The former Champ trained and guided Louisville's James Pritchard to a World Cruiserweight title and later a US Heavyweight title. He also continued singing in his successful Gospel group around the country.

Jimmy began to suffer from Dementia around 2004 and passed away on Tuesday, May 6, 2014, at the age of 74 in his hometown of Louisville, Kentucky. He was laid to rest in the Green Meadows Memorial Cemetery in Louisville, Kentucky.

MY OBSERVATION

Jimmy Ellis had one of the best personalities and dispositions of anyone that ever entered the ring. Jimmy trained as a youngster in Louisville, Kentucky, which is also my hometown, with others including, Cassius Clay, at the Columbia Gym. They were sparring partners, split wins as amateurs, and fought once as pros. Jimmy won a box-off tournament and ironically became the new World Heavyweight Champion immediately after Ali lost the title in 1967. Jimmy was part of my gym for many years and helped young people, including Louisville's James Pritchard to the World Cruiserweight Championship, have a better life to his very end. Jimmy is one of my most favorite Boxers and friends of all time!

JOE FRAZIER

"Smokin' Joe Frazier"

B: Jan. 12, 1944 D: Nov. 7, 2011
Born: Beaufort, South Carolina
5' 11" / 220 lbs.
Record: 32-4-1 27 KO's

Champion:
Feb. 16, 1970 - Jan. 22, 1973

Joseph William Frazier was the 12th child born to sharecroppers, Dolly Alston and Rubin Frazier, in Beaufort, South Carolina. They grew cotton and watermelons to feed and clothe the family. This happy family was very excited when they got their first TV in the 1950's. Joe's home was the place to be to watch the current shows, including their favorite, Boxing. He loved the sport so much that he made a makeshift training area for himself on the farm.

Joe, at a very young age, got different jobs, including a laborer at a Coca Cola plant and then some construction work. However, at a young fifteen years old, he thought that it was time to move on to the big city to gain more success and prosperity. He headed north and settled in Philadelphia, Pennsylvania where he began training in his passion more seriously.

Joe grew into a strong and powerful man who gathered an exceptional amateur record of 38 wins and only two losses. He also won The Golden Gloves Heavyweight Championship for 1962, 1963, and 1964. He was on the US Olympic coach's radar with a 38-2 record that didn't go unnoticed. Joe was chosen as an alternate at the Tokyo Olympic Games in Japan in 1964. Since teammate Buster Mathis had beaten Joe previously, he was chosen to represent the Heavyweight division. As fate would have it, Buster became injured at the last minute. This unfortunate event called on Joe to step up to represent America. Joe filled in and took on the Heavyweights from Uganda, Australia, Russia, and Germany. Victories over all opponents gave Joe Frazier the Heavyweight Gold Medal for the US in 1964.

Joe turned pro in 1965 and started strong with four wins by KO with little effort, and in 1966 he hooked up with famed trainer, Eddie Futch. Futch polished and perfected Joe's style of slipping, bobbing, and weaving to compete against the taller Boxers. Joe became the "Knockout King" as he won 8 of 9 wins by knockout in 1966, had 5 of 6 wins by knockout in 1967, 2 of 3 wins by knockout in 1968, and two knockouts in 1969. Joe also beat Buster Mathis as a professional and redeemed himself against his amateur loss to him in the early 1960s.

Joe earned his right to challenge the current Champion, Jimmy Ellis, on Monday, February 16, 1970, in Madison Square Garden. Joe was relentless against Ellis and won by a 5th round TKO. "Smokin" Joe Frazier was now the new Heavyweight Champion of the World!

Joe had one title defense against Bob Foster on November 18, 1970, at the Cobo Arena, in Detroit, Michigan. The contest was short with Joe winning a 2nd round knockout. However, undefeated Muhammad Ali was on the comeback trail and wanted his old title back. Undefeated Ali challenged undefeated Joe Frazier for the Undisputed World title. To the delight of the fans, both men put on a great show pounding each other for 15 rounds. This matchup was billed as the modern "Fight of The Century" at Madison Square Garden on Thursday, November 18, 1971. Boxing experts and fans would say it lived up to its expectations. After exchanging heavy leather for ten rounds, Joe wobbled

Ali in the 11th round and dropped him in the 15th to earn a Unanimous Decision to maintain his title. Both men spent time in the hospital following their battering to recover from the punishment. It was Ali's first pro defeat!

Joe climbed right back into the ring to stop two more opponents, Terry Daniels and Ron Stander in 1972. Next, the undefeated and Undisputed World Champion, Joe Frazier, took on much taller, bigger, and younger George Foreman. This title defense took place on Monday, January 22, 1973, at National Stadium in Kingston, Jamaica. The towering George Foreman dominated and dropped Joe six times before Referee Arthur Mercante stopped the one-sided affair in the 2nd round. It was Joe's first loss, and the World Heavyweight title now belonged to "Big" George Foreman.

Six months later saw Joe back in the ring against Joe Bugner in July 1973 in London, England. Joe won on points to get back on track and his goal to recapture the Heavyweight title.

Joe had three matches in 1974 beginning with his nemesis, Muhammad Ali, again in Madison Square Garden on Monday, January 28, 1974. The crowd expected another slugfest, and they got it. The two traded shots that again left them badly beaten and battered. However, this time, it was Ali who was awarded a 12-round Unanimous Decision.

Again, Joe bounced back into the ring six months later against a tough, Jerry Quarry. Joe took charge in this 5th round TKO rematch in the Madison Square Garden on June 17.

Joe's first bout of 1975 was also a 9th round TKO win over former Heavyweight Champion, Jimmy Ellis, on March 2 in Melbourne, Australia. His second and last bout this year was a "rubber match" with current Champion, Muhammad Ali. This bout was coined as the "Thrilla in Manilla", in the Philippines. As with many other opponents, Ali mocked and scorned Joe in the pre-fight build-up. The ridicule infuriated Joe, who never forgave Ali for his comments and expressions. However, the fight lived up to expectations, as it was a thriller that had both warriors slugging it out through 14 rounds. For Joe's safety, manager Eddie Futch had seen enough and stopped the brutal exchange before the 15th round to save the men from demise. Ali retained his title, but Joe didn't make it easy for him.

1976 only saw one bout for Joe, as once again he took on "Big" George Foreman, the man who took his title, on June 15 in New York. Joe, with a 32 and 3 record, did much better this time than their first bout. However, Joe was caught with a big left hook that stunned him, and after the second knockdown, the referee stopped the fight in the fifth round.

Joe was disappointed and decided to retire after this second loss to Foreman. He had only lost to two men, George Foreman and Muhammad Ali. However, five and a half years later, and at thirty-eight years old, Joe decided to come back to the ring. He had a bruising battle with Floyd Cummings in Chicago on

December 3, 1981. Joe managed to pull out a Draw, which proved to him that it was indeed time to retire for good.

After retirement, Joe stayed busy running his famous Boxing gym in Philly, training some Boxers, including his son, Marvis Frazier. He also had his own successful musical group, "Joe Frazier and the Knockouts." He appeared on several TV shows and had small parts in some movies. Joe also wrote an autobiography and a training book titled "Box Like the Pro's." To honor Joe and the others in the "Golden Age of Boxing," he was brought in to be photographed and a video made with four other Champions. The photoshoot and video were titled "Champions Forever." The group included Muhammad Ali, George Foreman, Kenny Norton, Larry Holmes, and himself. A rare event that included five of the greatest Boxers in history!

Joe lost much of his fortune with bad financial habits, including a land deal that he paid in a little over three-quarters of a million dollars. In this partner fiasco, he lost most of the money. Eventually, the land was sold without his knowledge or consent and is now worth 100 million dollars.

The International Boxing Research Organization rates Joe Frazier in the top ten Greatest Heavyweights of All Time. "The Ring" magazine ranked Joe the eighth "Greatest Heavyweight of all Time" and named him "Fighter of the Year" in 1967, 1970, and 1971. The "Boxing Writers Association of America" named him

"Fighter of the Year" in 1967, 1971, and 1975. Joe was also inducted into the International Boxing Hall of Fame in 1990.

Joe Frazier died of liver cancer on November 7, 2011, at the age of 67 in his hometown of Philadelphia, Pennsylvania. He was buried in Ivy Hill Cemetery in Alexandria, Virginia.

MY OBSERVATION

Joe Frazier was one of the busiest punchers of all time and can be compared to the heavyweight greats Jack Dempsey, Rocky Marciano, Sonny Liston and Mike Tyson. He never stopped bobbing, weaving, and punching. He played a significant part in Boxing history as the number one nemesis of Muhammad Ali. Their three bouts are considered some of the best contests in Boxing history. Joe lived Boxing until the very end!

GEORGE FOREMAN

"Big George" Foreman

B: Jan. 10, 1949
Born: Marshall, Texas
6' 4" / 230 lbs.
Record: Wins 76-5 68 KO's
"Over 50 KO Club"

Champion:
Jan. 22, 1973 - Oct. 5, 1974
Nov. 5, 1994 - Nov. 22, 1997

"Big" George Foreman was even big at birth as he weighed 10 pounds entering this world. He was the fourth of six children who grew up fighting in the ghettos of Houston, Texas, on a regular basis. Drinking and getting into trouble with police was also a regular occurrence. He didn't like school much and got terrible grades. When George got to junior high school, he decided to drop out. As his salvation, he found his way into the Job Corp at age 16. He learned many different construction trades there, including carpentry and bricklaying. He began to do so well that he became a Job Corp counselor.

George also began Boxing in the Corp while at a camp in Oregon in 1966. With his size and power, he became extremely formidable. As a great amateur, he topped his young career when he won the 1967 Nevada Golden Gloves title and the 1968 California Golden Gloves title. Also, in 1968, George won over Poland, Romania, Italy, and the Soviet Union to win the Olympic Gold Medal in Mexico City. To show his patriotism, he proudly waved his small American flag in the ring to show everyone the pride for his country.

George turned pro on June 23, 1969, and trained in the same gym as former Champion, Sonny Liston. It seemed as if he couldn't be stopped as he won 37 straight matches, annihilating 34 opponents. He was very active as he had 13 bouts in just the last six months of 1969. He added 12 more wins in 1970, 7 KO's in 1971, and five more KO's in 1972. George earned a title shot against WBA and WBC Champion, Joe Frazier on January 22, 1973, in Kingston, Jamaica. George went through Frazier with almost no opposition, knocking him down six times in the first round as he took the lineal title from Joe to become the 26th World Heavyweight Champion.

George defended his title once in 1973 on September 1 against Jose Roman in Tokyo, Japan. George had an easy win as he handed out another 1st round KO.

George looked unstoppable as he took on tough, Kenny Norton, who had broken Muhammad Ali's jaw just a year earlier. George had no problem handing Norton a 2nd round KO on March 26, 1974, in El Poliedro, Caracas.

George's impressive record caused a collision with the most flamboyant Boxer of the time, and former World Champion, Muhammad Ali. The most anticipated bout took place on October 30th, 1974 in Mai Kinshasa, Africa. It was billed as "The Rumble in The Jungle." George's size, power, and KO record made him the overwhelming favorite to win. As the bout began, George intended to end this thing early as he pounded Ali continuously with big bombs from both hands. Ali had a surprise for everyone as he pulled out his unique defensive strategy, now called, "Rope-A-Dope." George pounded Ali's body until he punched himself out. With little energy left, Ali turned on his offense and finished George off with a KO in the 8th round to stun the Boxing World. With this win, Ali then became the second man to regain the Heavyweight

Title in Boxing history. Floyd Patterson was the first man against Ingermar Johansson in 1960.

The loss to Muhammad Ali in Zaire was devastating to George as he left the ring for over a year. On January 24, 1976, George was presented with the opportunity to meet explosive, Ron Lyle for the vacant NABF Heavyweight title at Caesar's Palace in Las Vegas. It was a fascinating bout that had George knocking out Lyle in the 5th round. However, they dropped each other several times in a wild fourth round before George just outlasted Lyle. The NABF title belonged to George.

George picked up three more TKO's against Scott LaDoux, John Dino Denis, and Pedro Agosto before losing a disappointing and Unanimous Decision to veteran, Jimmy Young in San Juan, Puerto Rico. George retired after this bout at age 28...for ten full years.

George went home to Houston and became heavily involved in his church and the kids at the youth center there. He wanted to help kids become more successful and productive in life. Naturally, it took money to promote and progress his vision for the kids in Houston. So, George climbed back into the ring at 38 years old when most Boxers are retiring for good. However, George was not like most other Boxers! His new found personality and vision won him much fame and favor. He defied age and reason with 15 knockouts of the next 24 opponents in the next three years.

George became a national icon and landed much TV

exposure through guest appearances, commercials, and, ultimately, the famous George Foreman Grill. After three years of wins, George earned a shot at Evander Holyfield and the IBF, WBA, and the WBC World Heavyweight title belts in Atlantic City. He had a good showing against the much younger man, but Holyfield was awarded a Unanimous Decision over George.

Determined, 42-year-old George Foreman, climbed back into the ring eight months later against former Heavyweight Champion, Jimmy Ellis in Reno, Nevada. George stopped Ellis with a TKO for his first win after the Holyfield loss. George won two more matches in 1992 and 1993 against Alex Stewart and Pierre Coetzer in Nevada. George got another shot at the new and vacant WBO Heavyweight title on June 7, 1993, in Las Vegas. It was against Tommy Morrison, the nephew of the famous actor, John Wayne. It was another disappointment for George losing to the much younger, 24-year-old slugger.

No, the nearly 46-year-old former World Heavyweight Champion did not have a second retirement on his mind. George's very next bout was in Las Vegas against another 26-year-old, Michael Moorer, who possessed the IBF and WBA titles. November 5, 1994, belonged to George, as he had finally regained his title after knocking out Moorer in the 10th round. George became the third man to regain the World Heavyweight Title and the oldest to hold that title in Boxing history.

George defended his titles, and with the WBU title on the line, he took on German Axel Shulz and won a Majority Decision on April 1995. He put his titles on the line and was in pursuit of the vacant International Boxing Association belt that was up for grabs against Crawford Grimsley on November 3, 1996. George pulled off another win with a Unanimous Decision to retain the combinations of belts. Lou Savarese also lost in Atlantic City in a Split Decision to the 48-year-old Champion on April 26, 1997.

George astounded Boxing fans as he took on another 26-year-old hard-hitting, Brooklyn born, Shannon Briggs. George stood his ground, fought like a Champ, but sadly lost in a Majority Decision to Briggs on November 22, 1997. George decided it was the right time to retire as a two-time World Champion, oldest to hold the title at 46 years old, and a rich and famous man!

However, George only retired from inside the ring. He kept busy as a color commentator on HBO and was on many TV ads and shows, one being his own TV show called "George." He also wrote his own bestselling autobiography. Naturally, he stayed busy at his church and the youth center. He also made a large amount of money with his "George Foreman Grill," earning him over 150 million dollars, more than his Boxing career, with a lot less punishment.

"The Ring" magazine featured George many times, including "Fighter of the Year," "Ninth Greatest Puncher of All Time," and "The Fourth Greatest

Heavyweight of All Time." He was also inducted into The International Hall of Fame in 2003.

George has five sons, all named "George," and one daughter, Freda. George no.3 and Freda also boxed professionally.

George Foreman is one of the wealthiest Boxers of all time with a reported current net worth of 250 million dollars. He is also one of America's most notable and loved celebrities!

MY OBSERVATION

George Foreman is one of the most iconic and revered Boxers of the 20th century. He actually had two Boxing careers. His first go-around was a fearsome disposition to all opponents with his bad demeanor and attitude. He was a mountain of a man that seemingly couldn't be beaten early in his career. That is until the underdog, Muhammad Ali, met him in Zaire. This outcome shocked the fans and experts, and even George couldn't believe it.

He retired sometime afterwards and became involved heavily in his church and youth group. Needing funds to support his beloved children's recreation center, he returned to the ring simply for the paydays. Religion and the youth center brought George back to Boxing. He was a new man with a lovable personality that the TV and fans couldn't get enough of. He became the World Champion again and also earned millions from his endorsements deals which included the "George Foreman Grill."

He has a very likable personality and disposition that would attract anyone. He's a person who would be just fun to hang out with!

LEON SPINKS

"Neon Leon"

B: July 11, 1953
D: February 5, 2021
Born: St. Louis, Missouri
6' 1" / 190 lbs.
Record: 26-17-3 14 KO'S

Champion:
Feb. 15, 1978 - Sept. 15, 1978

Leon Spinks was the older brother to Michael, and together they were the only brothers to both win Olympic Gold Medals and World Heavyweight titles! Leon won the 1974 World Amateur title in the Light Heavyweight division in Havana, Cuba. He also won in the same division in 1975 in Mexico City, Mexico. Leon won Gold as a Light Heavyweight, while the younger brother, Michael, won Gold in the Middleweight division at the 1976 Montreal Summer Olympics. Leon won over Morocco, The Soviet Union, East Germany, Poland, and Cuba that year. Leon also won the World Heavyweight Professional title in 1978 over Heavyweight Muhammad Ali.

Leon was born in St. Louis, Missouri, and boxed while serving in the US Marine Corp. He had a good amateur record and turned pro in 1977. Oddly, in 1978, only after seven professional wins, undefeated Leon, challenged Champion, Muhammad Ali, for "The World Heavyweight Championship" title. As the underdog, Boxing fans were extremely shocked when Leon became the first Light Heavyweight in history to challenge a Heavyweight and win. He was also the only man to take the World Title from Muhammad Ali. Leon won the bout by a Split Decision in Las Vegas, Nevada, on February 15, 1978.

However, Ali was not going to let a youngster like Leon Spinks keep his title very long. They met again precisely seven months later in the New Orleans "Superdome" on September 15, 1978. Ali controlled the action this time as he avenged his loss to Leon with a 15 round Unanimous Decision. This return win boasted Ali to become the only man to be a "Three Time Lineal World Heavyweight Champion." Feeling vindicated, Ali retired after this fight. However, like many Boxers before him, he returned for more action, but only had two more bouts against Larry Holmes and Trevor Berbick.

Leon's very next contest was also a loss. It was a 1st round TKO to Gerrie Coetzee of South Africa in Monaco. After these losses, he started a string of more wins than losses. Oddly, after being at the very top, Leon lost to top-ranked Boxers as well as some journeymen fighters just to make a living.

Leon's next big chance for the title was against current Champion, Larry Holmes, at the Joe Louis Arena in Detroit, Michigan, on Friday, June 12, 1981. Leon couldn't handle Holmes' blistering jabs and cannon like right hands. Leon was stopped in the 3rd round with a TKO. Ironically, younger brother Michael, later won over the Champion Larry Holmes to take the title and block him from matching the undefeated, Rocky Marciano's record of 49-0.

Leon won seven more bouts with only one loss that included the vacant NABF Cruiserweight title against Jesse Burnett on October 31, 1982, at the Great Gorge Resort in New Jersey. He also won the WBC Continental Americas Heavyweight title against Kip Keneat at the Felt Forum in New York on December 13, 1985.

Leon lost his title during a string of no wins in

nine contests, except for recapturing his Continental title against Jeff Jordan in Japan on April 28, 1987. Again, Leon went on a five-bout winning streak before bouncing back and forth with wins and losses. He faced Fred Houpe and lost a Unanimous Decision on his very last Heavyweight bout on December 4, 1995, in his hometown of St. Louis, Missouri.

Leon was an all-around competitor who tried Wrestling after Boxing. Coincidentally, Leon agreed to the "Boxer versus Wrestler" with Japanese Wrestler, Antonio Inoki, the same opponent that Ali unsuccessfully faced. Naturally, it was a clumsy matchup, with Leon losing this "apple and oranges" contest. However, Leon did win the Frontier WWA World Martial Arts World title in March 1992. With this title, he became the second man to win world titles in both Boxing and Wrestling. The other man to accomplish this was Primo Canera.

Leon fell on hard times and moved around the country and did odd jobs to earn a living. He was a restaurant greeter, YMCA worker, did after school programs, and started a gym in Detroit. Unfortunately, he developed some health issues as he was diagnosed with brain trauma in 2012. In addition, he was also in a coma for some time due to complications with his intestines. Leon's health is now better, and he resides in Las Vegas, Nevada.

Leon had two sons that also successfully boxed. Leon Calvin and Cory who became a Welterweight and Junior Middleweight Champion. Sadly, Calvin was murdered in 1990 as he was driving home in East St. Louis.

Leon was on the cover of Sports Illustrated in 1978 and inducted into the Nevada Hall of Fame in 2017 along with his younger brother, Michael Spinks.

MY OBSERVATION

Leon Spinks was one of two brothers who first won Olympic Gold medals in Boxing in the same year. Their medals were earned in the Summer Games in 1976, held in Montreal, Canada. Their second feat was also the first brothers to both win World Heavyweight Boxing Championship titles. Leon's claim to fame was beating Champion Muhammad Ali, and Michael's was beating Champion Larry Holmes. They both had awkward styles and threw many punch combinations. You can't talk about Boxing history without mentioning the Spinks brothers.

KENNY NORTON

B: Aug. 9, 1943 D: Sept. 18, 2013
Born: Jacksonville, FL.
6' 3" / 210 lbs.
Record 42-7-1 33 KO's

Champion:
March 3, 1973 - Sept.10, 1973
March 18, 1978 - June 9, 1978

Kenny Howard Norton was the son of John and Ruth Norton of Jacksonville, Illinois. Kenny was an outstanding athlete who played football and was part of the Track and Field team in high school. As a senior in 1960, he entered all eight-track and field events and won seven of the eight categories. Kenny then made history as the State of Illinois quickly changed the rules to only permitting a student to enter no more than four events at once. Kenny's skills and talents also earned him a football scholarship to Northeast Missouri State University.

After college, Kenny joined the US Marine Corp, and in 1963 took up Boxing and competed in the military for the next four years. His great athleticism earned him a 24-2 amateur record and three "All Marine Heavyweight" titles. He also won the North Carolina AAU Golden Gloves title, International AAU title, and the Pan American title. Kenny was declared the best Boxer to ever compete for the Marine Corp with his unique "cross-armed" defensive style. This style was a favorite of other Champions, including Archie Moore, Joe Frazier, and George Foreman.

Kenny turned pro in 1967 and won his first thirty fights, including a win over "The Greatest," Muhammad Ali, his second loss. Twenty-three of Ken's first thirty wins were TKO or KO's over his opponents. Boxing fans were shocked when Kenny, a 5 to 1 underdog took the NABF Heavyweight crown and handed Ali a Split Decision loss. Kenny also gave Ali a broken jaw in the 11th round on March 31, 1973, in the Sports Arena in San Diego, California. However, six months later, in a rematch, Ali took the NABF title from Kenny with a very controversial Split Decision. This took place at the "Forum" in Inglewood, California, on September 10, 1973.

Kenny's luck didn't get better as he next met "Big" George Foreman for the Undisputed Heavyweight title in Caracas, Venezuela, on March 26, 1974. The undefeated, Foreman made short work of Kenny as the fight was stopped and called a TKO for Foreman in the 2nd round. George Foreman was now the new World Heavyweight Champion. Kenny carried on and won his next ten bouts except for his third and final bout with Muhammad Ali.

Kenny met Ali for their third bout on September 28, 1976, in Yankee Stadium. By this time, Ali had upset George Foreman in the famous "Rumble in the Jungle." Ali put his titles on the line against Kenny, whom he had lost one and won one. This bout was another physical slugfest that had Ali winning another controversial Unanimous Decision. Experts ranked this bout as the "Tenth Greatest bout of All Time."

Kenny fought three times in 1977, winning all three before meeting Larry Holmes on June 9, 1978, at Caesars Palace. Holmes held the WBA Heavyweight title at that time, and Kenny owned the WBC version and put it on the line. It was a slugfest and, Kenny was very disappointed as he lost a Split Decision and his WBC title after 15 rounds.

With no more title shots, Kenny won two more bouts against top talent, Randy Stephens and Randall "Tex" Cobb. However, Kenny lost two bouts against tough, Earnie Shavers and Gerry Cooney, and then a Draw with Scott LeDoux in the next three years.

Kenny retired at the age of nearly 38 years old in 1981. He stayed connected outside the ring as a color commentator at Boxing shows, appeared in "Champions Forever," appeared on TV and in movies, including the hit movie, "Mandingo." He was booked for many speaking engagements, published an autobiography, and started a management company to help other athletes.

Kenny had five children, including Kenny Norton Jr., who played football at UCLA, in the NFL, and starred in three "Superbowl's." Kenny Jr. was also a coach at the University of Southern California, for the Seattle Seahawks and Oakland Raiders.

Kenny had a great personality and disposition who was significantly liked by his fans and opponents. He was ranked as the "Twenty-Second Greatest Heavyweight of All Time" and was inducted into the International Boxing Hall of Fame in 1992.

Sadly, Kenny was involved in a severe car accident in 1986, in which he never fully recovered. He also suffered a series of strokes as his health deteriorated. He passed away at a care facility in Las Vegas on September 18, 2013, at age 70. Kenny Norton was buried in his hometown at Jacksonville East Cemetery in Jacksonville, Illinois.

MY OBSERVATION

Kenny Norton was a highly educated man who excelled in many sports, including Boxing. He had a great disposition who was liked by all, including his opponents. He beat the great Muhammad Ali once and lost two very close and controversial rematches to him. This must put him at the top of any records and statistics. Actually, most of the seven bouts that he lost were all very close or controversial. I was fortunate enough to meet him in Las Vegas. He was very gracious and autographed a photo of us for our Boxing gym. Kenny is one of my all-time favorites!

LARRY HOLMES

"The Easton Assassin"

B: Nov. 3, 1949
Born: Easton, Pennsylvania
6' 3" / 220 lbs.
Record: 69-6 44 KO's

Champion:
June 9, 1980 - May 20,1985

Larry Holmes was one of a dozen children to John and Flossie Holmes of Easton, Pennsylvania. The family survived on welfare and what his father made as a gardener. Like some other former Champions, Larry quit school in the seventh grade to work odd jobs and help support his family.

Larry started Boxing at 19 years old and had a winning amateur record in the late 1960s and early 1970s with only three losses. Like some other future Champions, he competed in the Olympic trials but wasn't successful in 1972. Larry decided it was time to earn some money and turned professional in 1973. He ultimately became a sparring partner for Muhammad Ali, Joe Frazier, and others. He believed if he could hang in there and train with the best, he would be successful one day. He worked very hard for five long years and ultimately won a Unanimous Decision over Earnie Shavers. This earned him a meeting with then Champion, Kenny Norton, on Friday, June 9, 1978, in Las Vegas. The fight was close, but Larry pulled out a late Split Decision win in the fifteen rounder. Larry Holmes became the 29th and new World Heavyweight Champion!

Next, Larry defended his title against Alfredo Evangelista, Ossie Ocasio, Mike Weaver, a rematch with Earnie Shavers, Lorenzo Simpson, Leroy Jones, Scott LeDoux and several other top contenders.

Nearly 41-year-old Muhammad Ali came out of retirement to take on Larry with a four-time Heavyweight title on his mind on Thursday, October 2, 1980. This contest was billed as the "Last Hurrah"! Ali's sluggish, defensive performance certainly didn't reflect the spirited Ali of old. Thirty-one-year-old Larry took charge from the opening bell and was given very little opposition. Ali didn't offer his usual quality performance, so trainer, Angelo Dundee, decided to step in and stop the bout after the 10th round. It was another win that maintained Larry's perfect record. Actually, a medical exam after the fight showed the beginning signs of Ali's health deterioration and what came to be more severe problems. Larry said that he was saddened to be the one to beat "The Greatest" while he was in his decline, much like the Rocky Marciano over "The Brown Bomber," Joe Louis on October 26, 1951.

Larry added eight more KO's and a Trevor Berbick Decision on April 11, 1981, before being challenged by Leon Spinks, the former World Heavyweight Champion for his title. Larry made short work of Leon as he TKO'd him in just three rounds. Larry Holmes was still the Undisputed World Heavyweight Champion.

Larry won ten tough title defenses before meeting Leon's younger, 21-year-old brother, Michael Spinks. They met at the Riviera Hotel in Las Vegas on Monday, May 20, 1985. Larry, nearly 36 years old, put his 48-0 perfect record on the line. If Larry could have won this bout, he would have tied the Legendary and Undefeated Rocky Marciano. Rocky, who was the only Champion to retire undefeated with a 49-0 record. Unbelievably, Larry lost his title in a very controversial, Unanimous Decision to a very disagreeing crowd. There had been much contention between Larry and the promoter, Don King, before and after this production. One might wonder if this had any effect on Larry this night?

Larry met Michael Spinks in a rematch on April 19, 1986, for a chance to regain his title at the Las Vegas Hilton. It was another loss and disappointment for Larry via a controversial Split Decision in which the crowd also loudly, disagreed. Larry decided to retire after these two controversial events.

Nearly two years later, 39-year-old Larry was lured out of retirement to take on a 21-year-old, Mike Tyson. This contest was for the WBA, WBC, and IBF Heavyweight Championship of the World and 2.8 million dollars. If Larry could have won this bout, he would also be a two-time World Heavyweight Champion. However, it wasn't to be. The young, Mike Tyson was just too much for the older Larry Holmes. Larry was KO'd in the fourth round and decided to retire from the ring, but just for three years.

The competitor in Larry brought him back to the ring on April 7, 1991, against little known, Tim Anderson. Larry stopped Anderson with a first-round TKO to begin a string of six wins before one more shot at the Undisputed Heavyweight title. The task was against a very tough and versatile, Evander Holyfield from Atlanta, Georgia. The bout took place in Caesar's Palace on June 19, 1992. Larry was 43 years old and one of the oldest in Boxing history trying to regain the Heavyweight title. Larry held his own, but just couldn't overcome the much younger Holyfield. Larry lost a Unanimous Decision to the thirty-year-old Champion.

Without slowing, Larry continued his craft winning seven straight bouts before meeting Oliver McCall for the WBC version of the Heavyweight Championship. The match took place at Caesars Palace on April 8, 1995, when he was 46 years old. However, another title slipped away as McCall won a 12 round Decision over Larry. After four more wins, Larry was offered another chance at a title by the IBO version against Brian Nielsen in Brondby Hall in Copenhagen, Denmark. Forty-eight-year-old Larry fought his best against the much younger opponent, but again came up short with a Split Decision loss against Nielsen.

Larry climbed back through the ropes four more times to win every bout, including his last against "Toughman" contest sensation and now pro Boxer, Eric "Butterbean" Esch in Norfolk, Virginia on July 27, 2002. Larry won this bout by a ten round Unanimous Decision and decided to call it quits at the age of fifty-three and one-half years old and his seventy-fifth bout.

Larry was a shrewd businessman and invested his money well back at his hometown of Easton, Pennsylvania, in real estate and businesses. He became one of the most financially successful Boxers to maintain and grow his earnings. He also was successful as a talk show host, a color commentator, and continued to promote Boxing in many other ways.

Larry is best known for having one of the best jabs and right cross combinations in Boxing history with twenty successful title defenses. He had the most defenses behind Joe Louis and Wladimir Klitschko as the longest-reigning Champion.

Larry Holmes was a highly marketable opponent who the fans loved to watch and is viewed as one of the greatest Heavyweight Champions of all time. He was inducted into the International Boxing Hall of Fame in 2008.

MY OBSERVATION

Larry Holmes is one of my favorite World Champions! He had an impressive cannon like jab and a thundering right cross that his opponents never saw coming. He was wise to train and spar with the Champions early in his career, which helped him to become the future Champion. He had one of the longest reigns in Boxing history and in my opinion, should have tied and surpassed Rocky Marciano's undefeated record. Larry also wisely invested his earnings well and lives comfortably today in Easton, Pennsylvania. Larry was definitely a Boxing superstar!

MICHAEL SPINKS

"Jinx Spinks"

B: July 13, 1956
Born: St. Louis, Missouri
6' 2" / 212 lbs.
Record: 31-1 21 KO's

Champion:
Lt. Heavy Mar.18, 1983 - Sep.21, 1985
Heavyweight Sep.21, 1985 - June 27, 1988

Boxing was in the blood of the Spinks family as Michael and older brother, Leon; both became World Heavyweight Champions. Michael's nephew, Cory, would also become the Welterweight and Light Middleweight World Champion.

Michael followed in his brother's footsteps in Boxing as he won the Middleweight Golden Gloves title in Denver in 1974. He also won a Silver Medal in the National Golden Gloves AAU Middleweight title in 1975, and the 1976 National Golden Gloves title.

Michael and older brother, Leon both competed in the 1976 Montreal Summer Olympics in Boxing. Michael won the Middleweight Gold, and Leon won the Light Heavyweight Gold. They are the only brothers in Boxing history to win the Gold in the same Olympics and become professional Heavyweight Boxing Champions.

Michael continued to compete and developed into a successful Light Heavyweight while working a regular job in St. Louis. He eventually amassed a 93-7 amateur record with 35 KO's before turning pro in 1977. He won all six bouts that year with KO's and Decisions.

Michael only had two bouts in 1978, winning both before just one victory in 1979. He was busier in 1980, winning all five matches that year. Michael won over all four opponents in 1981, including Eddie Mustafa Muhammad in Las Vegas for the WBA Light Heavyweight title. Michael won that bout by a Unanimous Decision at the Imperial Palace Hotel and Casino. In Las Vegas, the New York Champion had one title defense in 1981 in which he TKO'd Vonzell Johnson in the 7th round.

Michael defended his title four times in Atlantic City, New Jersey, in 1982, winning all bouts by TKO. After 23 professional wins, Michael met Dwight Muhammad Qawi at the Convention Hall in Atlantic City to defend his WBA title on March 18, 1983. It was also his attempt to become the Undisputed Light Heavyweight World Champion. Michael did it; he won the Undisputed Light Heavyweight Championship after 23 wins. The new Champion defended his title once more in 1983 against Oscar Rivadeneyra in Vancouver, Canada, with a TKO win in the tenth round. Michael also defended his title once in 1984 and twice in 1985 with TKOs before moving up to the Heavyweight division and challenging Champion Larry Holmes for the Undisputed Heavyweight title. The bout took place at the Riviera Hotel in Las Vegas on September 21, 1985. Michael was putting his undefeated 28-0 record against Holmes's unbeaten 48-0 record.

Much leather was exchanged in this Don King production, and it appeared that Holmes was in control and would match the Rocky Marciano's 49-0 record. However, when the results were revealed, Michael was awarded the win by Unanimous Decision. Boxing fans on hand disagreed and showed their disapproval right away. Not only did Holmes have his first loss, but he would never match Rocky Marciano's undefeated record. Michael's very next bout was a rematch with now the former Champion, Larry Holmes, on April 1986 at the Las Vegas Hilton. As this contest unveiled, the fans believed surely the judges would declare Holmes the winner this time. Not so, Michael was awarded the rematch by a Split Decision to retain his Undisputed World Heavyweight title. Michael defended his crown once more in 1986 and once in 1987 against Gerry Cooney in Atlantic City on June 15. Michael was victorious again with a 5th round TKO to remain Champion.

Michael reigned one more full year before being challenged by Boxing sensation, "Iron" Mike Tyson for the WBA, WBC, IBF, and "The Ring" lineal titles. This was another bout between two undefeated contestants as they met in Atlantic City on June 27, 1988. Michael never got started as Tyson dropped him twice before knocking him out at the halfway mark in the first round. That was Michael's first loss on his record after ten title defenses. He handed over all of his titles to Mike Tyson that night, then retired the next day.

Michael set another record as he was the first undefeated Light Heavyweight Champion to beat an Undefeated Heavyweight Champion, which was Larry Holmes. "The Ring magazine," (which is the Boxing bible), and The International Boxing Research Organization ranked Michael as the third "Greatest Light Heavyweight Champion of all Time," just behind Ezzard Charles and Archie Moore. Michael was inducted into the International Boxing Hall of Fame in 1994.

It's not likely we'll ever again see two brothers who both won Olympic Gold Medals in the same year, and then both go on to become World Heavyweight Champions!

Michael is currently living in Wilmington, Delaware, where he makes some public appearances, visits schools, and passes on his expertise and experience to young Boxers.

Michael experienced some financial problems when his longtime friend and manager, Butch Lewis, passed away in 2011. They had a unique agreement in which Lewis would handle Michael's financial affairs indefinitely. However, after Lewis' passing, Michael surprisingly found that Lewis had questionable management practices that cost him some of his savings. Attorneys that inherited Michael's arrangement also seemed to cause problems and complications to his wealth, which cost him even more of his earnings.

Michael and Leon Spinks gave the Boxing world many fun and exciting displays of their talents.

MY OBSERVATION

Michael's significant accomplishments were winning an Olympic Gold Medal, becoming the first Undefeated Light Heavyweight Champion, and first Light Heavyweight Champion to beat the Heavyweight Champion! He was a very mobile Boxer who could punch from many different angles with many combinations. This made it very awkward for his opponents, including Champion, Larry Holmes, whom he blocked from tying Rocky Marciano's perfect, 49-0 undefeated record. Michael met Holmes in a rematch seven months later and was awarded another exciting and controversial decision.

MIKE TYSON

"Iron" Mike Tyson

B. June 30, 1966
Born: Brooklyn, New York
5' 10" / 210 lbs.
Record: 50-6-2 44 KO's

Champion:
Nov. 22, 1986 - Feb.11, 1990
March 16, 1996 - Nov. 9, 1996

Mike Gerald Tyson grew up in the tough neighborhood of Brownsville in Brooklyn, New York. He used his fists a few times as anyone would in this part of the city. He eventually became a student of the legendary Boxing trainer, Cus D'Amato. Cus had also led another young man, Floyd Patterson, to the Heavyweight Boxing Championship in 1956. Mike, like Patterson, developed the "Peek a Boo" defensive style that could be effective for a shorter or smaller person. This style was a very effective way to get in close to your opponent without getting hit squarely. As Mike continued to win, he became a very feared and successful amateur cutting through opponents like butter. He tallied a winning record, including gold medals in 1981 and 1982, in the Junior Olympics.

Mike turned pro in 1985 and cruised through 15 bouts, sparing no one. He won twenty-six of his first twenty-eight bouts by KO or TKO. Sadly, his trainer and mentor, Cus D'Amato, died in November of that year, leaving the question of how it would affect Mike's mindset and performances? However, his march continued in 1986 with eight more wins, and on November 22, he met WBC Champ, Trevor Berbick, for his Championship belt. Mike TKO'd Berbick in the second round to become the youngest man in history to win that version of the Heavyweight title at 20 years old, just ahead of Muhammad Ali.

On March 7, 1987, Mike went in search of WBA Champ James "Bonecrusher" Smith's version of the title and took it with a 12-round Unanimous Decision in Las Vegas. Only five months later, on August 1, 1987, Mike challenged Tony Tucker for his IBF version of the title in Las Vegas. Mike took this third most important division of the Heavyweight title to become the first man to hold all three Heavyweight belts. Mike finished out 1987 with a 7th round TKO over former Gold Medalist, Tyrell Biggs.

Former Champ, Larry Holmes fell first in January 1988 in a fourth-round knockout, and incidentally, this was Holmes' only KO loss in 75 bouts. Next, Tony Tubbs also dropped in Tokyo, Japan, on March 21 of that year, by a TKO in the second round. Now, the big prize was the meeting of lineal Champ, Michael Spinks. Spinks had taken the lineal title from Larry Holmes in Las Vegas on September 21, 1985. This Tyson-Spinks championship bout took place at the Convention Hall in Atlantic City, New Jersey. Experts thought this matchup would be a very strategic battle, but became one of Mike's easiest wins with a 91 second KO in the first round. Mike had now earned the lineal Championship and became recognized as the 31st Undisputed Heavyweight Champion of the World on June 27, 1988.

The same year turned out to be a problematic year for Mike. He didn't have the guidance of Cus D'Amato, did have problems with manager Bill Cayton, fired Kevin Rooney, and got a divorce from actress Robin Givens. Unbelievably, these things didn't slow his winning streak this year or in 1989!

Tyson only had two title defenses in 1989, knocking

out British Champ, Frank Bruno in the fifth round and Carl "The Truth" Williams in the first round, in July.

Mike, under new management, met lesser-known contender, James "Buster" Douglas in Tokyo, Japan, on February 11, 1990. Douglas was a 42 to 1 underdog and wasn't given much of a chance by experts or fans. Maybe, Mike took this underdog too lightly even though Douglas had a 13-inch reach advantage to keep him away. As the match began, Douglas fired jabs continuously. Douglas knew Mike's style had always been to go right through his opponent. Douglas also knew what he had to do. He had to keep Mike away until just the right time. Like most other opponents, Mike floored Douglas, but he got right back up. Things turned around, and this time Douglas caught the approaching Mike with an uppercut punch. Douglas followed with relenting combinations to unbelievably take Mike out in the 10th round. The impossible happened! Mike lost his titles after five years of being undefeated and seemingly invincible. It was a shocking upset to the Boxing experts and fans around the world.

Mike got back in the gym in 1990 and came out swinging as he took out Henry Tillman by KO and Alex Stewart by TKO. On June 28, 1991, Tyson took on Donovan "Razor" Ruddock in Las Vegas. It seemed to be an even match until the referee controversially stepped in and stopped the bout in the 7th round and awarded Mike the victory. The crowd was very unhappy and loudly protested this early stoppage. To settle things, several months later, a rematch was on between the two. This time, Mike proved to be the victor in a 12 round Unanimous Decision. In 1992, Mike faced some legal trouble and was away from Boxing for nearly four years.

Mike got right back to it in 1995 with his first fight against Peter McNeely. Boxing fans welcomed Mike back with a ninety-six million-dollar PPV gate. Mike won, but by Disqualification over McNeely in the first round. Next, Buster Mathis fell in March 1996, and later Mike took on British and WBC Heavyweight Champ, Frank Bruno. Mike made short work of Bruno in a 3rd round KO to take that title. WBA titleholder, Bruce Seldon also relinquished his title to Mike in the first round on September 7, 1996. When Mike recaptured these titles, he joined the elite club to win titles two times. One last contest of 1996 in November was against another underdog, Evander "The Real Deal" Holyfield. Mike put up his WBA title as the fans saw a great match. The bout was stopped in the 11th round as Holyfield was just too much for Mike on this night. This win made Holyfield one of very few men in history to win a major Heavyweight Championship three times.

Eager to win back his crown, Mike faced Holyfield on June 28, 1997, for a highly anticipated rematch at the MGM in Las Vegas. It was another exciting slugfest that became one for the history books. Unbelievably, Mike pulled out a street fighting tactic and bit Holyfield's ear in the 3rd round during a clinch. Referee Mills Lane halted the fight and took two points from

Mike's scorecard. No one could believe their eyes and were stunned when Mike repeated the act. The second time, Mike actually bit part of Holyfield's ear entirely off in the same round. Mills Lane could see no more, and disqualified Mike and awarded Holyfield the win. Mike claims that Holyfield was head butting in this bout as he did in their first matchup without any consequences. It's reported that this bout earned Mike 100 million dollars and Holyfield 35 million, which was the highest-grossing bout to date. It was also the first Heavyweight title fight to end in Disqualification since Max Schmeling won over Jack Sharkey by a low blow in the 4th round on June 12, 1930. Mike was fined three million dollars and lost his Boxing license for the unsportsmanship. Mike's Boxing license was returned in October 1998, and he took on South African, Francois Botha at the MGM in Las Vegas. Botha was outpointing Mike until he caught Botha with a devastating right hand and KO'd him at the end of the 5th round. A year later, Mike faced the law again and was away for nine more months this time. Mike then wasted no time in his comeback as he took on Orlin Norris in 1999. Mike dropped Norris, which caused him to twist his ankle and could not continue. The decision was ruled a "No Contest."

Mike had three bouts in 2000, winning all by Knockout. Julius Francis fell in the 2nd round in Manchester, England in January, and Lou Savarese was dropped in the 1st round in Glasgow, England, in June of that year. In October, Mike did severe damage to Andrew Golota, to stop him in the third round. Brian Nielsen lost by a TKO in Copenhagen, Denmark, in 2001, as this was Mike's only fight that year.

Mike, now age 35, met British and Undisputed World Champion, Lennox Lewis for the WBC, IBF, and IBO lineal titles at the Pyramid Arena in Memphis, Tennessee on June 8, 2002. Mike was older and maybe a bit slower, as he lost to Lewis in the 8th by Knockout. Even with a loss, this event was the largest pay per view in history at 110 million dollars. However, Mike came right back to take out Clifford Etienne in the first round by KO in February 2003 for Mike's only bout that year. Again, only one bout in 2004 against Englishman Danny Williams in July in Louisville, Kentucky. Mike was KO'd in the fourth round, but suffered a torn knee ligament, which surely affected his performance.

After knee surgery, Mike came back for what would be his very last contest against Kevin McBride in Washington, D.C., on June 11, 2005. They were trading punches when Mike oddly announced that he wasn't coming back out for the 7th round. He merely said that he didn't want to box anymore!

In 2006, Mike needed income, so he did some exhibition bouts. He earned almost 66 million dollars that year but was deeply in debt. Unbelievably, he had very little left after earning $700 million in his career. He was millions in debt and decided to declare bankruptcy.

After retiring from the ring, Mike kept busy doing

commercials, TV interviews, movie parts, and a one-man show that he performed in Las Vegas, on Broadway, and on HBO. This documentary show he called "Undisputed Truth" was also available on" YouTube."

Mike is still a "larger than life" character who holds one of the longest unified championships reigns with eight consecutive defenses. Joe Louis, Wladimir Klitschko, Larry Holmes, and Muhammad Ali are the Champions with the most title defenses.

Mike is compared to the greatest Boxers of all time, such as Jack Dempsey, Joe Louis, Rocky Marciano, and Muhammad Ali. He is also ranked as one of the hardest hitters of all time and was inducted into the International Hall of Fame and the World Hall of Fame in 2011.

Mike was married three times, fathered seven children, and lives in Seven Hills, Nevada. It's reported that his current net worth is three million dollars after earning an astounding 700 million dollars during his career.

MY OBSERVATION

Mike is known as the fearless Boxing machine that cut through his opponents like butter! He was a most exciting person during his career. I and everyone else was anxious to see what he would do next. He studied Boxing from Cus D'Amato, a Boxing historian. This knowledge gave him a skill set, which was a very systematic approach to the art and science of Boxing. He also had an extreme training regime that led him to the top. He had a roller coaster life, but became the Heavyweight Champion and much more in life. He is in the league of best punchers of all time with Jack Dempsey, Joe Louis, Rocky Marciano, Sonny Liston, and Joe Frazier. I believe Mike is the best inside fighter of all time. I also believe he will show up again in the square ring.

JAMES DOUGLAS

"Buster" Douglas

B: April 7, 1960
Born: Columbus, Ohio
6' 4" / 230 lbs.
Record: 38-6-1-1 25 KO's

Champion:
Feb.1, 1990 - Oct. 25, 1990

James "Buster" Douglas was born to Lula Pearl and William "Dynamite" Douglas of Columbus,

Ohio, in 1960. Buster's father "Billy" was a Boxer in the Middleweight and Light Heavyweight divisions in the 1960s and 1970s. He also took on the best opponents of the day. Naturally, Billy trained and managed Buster for much of his career.

Buster was a natural athlete who attended Linden McKinley High School and played football and basketball there. His talents led his high school to a AAA Basketball Championship in 1977. Buster played ball at Coffeyville College where he was inducted into their Hall of Fame. Later, he also starred at Sinclair Community College and Mercyhurst University.

Buster began Boxing at the age of ten in Columbus, Ohio, and had a good amateur career. So, with his potential, experience, and guidance, he and his father thought that it was time to turn pro in May of 1981. Douglas won his first twenty bouts, lost only one to David Bey, won the next six contests, and earned a draw against Steffen Tangstad of Denmark. He had another string of wins, which included journeymen, contenders, and former Champions.

On February 11, 1990, Buster got a big chance against 37-0, undefeated Champion, Mike Tyson in the Tokyo Dome, in Tokyo, Japan. Buster was a 42-1 underdog, and hardly anyone gave him a chance. However, he was in top shape physically and mentally needed to succeed while Tyson was maybe off his game. It was great boxing as Buster kept Tyson away with jabs that had a 12 inch reach advantage. Explosive punches were exchanged until Tyson dropped Buster in the 8th round. It seemed that Buster would be just another victim of Tyson's. However, unlike most other opponents of Tyson's, Buster got back up with even more determination. The 9th was just the opposite; this round showed Buster in complete control. Buster tried, but just couldn't finish Tyson in this round. However, the 10th round was payday for Buster when he caught Tyson forging in. Buster landed his uppercut and stunned and wobbled Tyson. Buster then capitalized as he added a fierce combination of punches to shockingly end Tyson's night in the 10th round. The "underdog" James "Buster" Douglas was now the 32nd lineal and Undisputed IBF, WBA, and WBC Heavyweight Boxing Champion of the World.

Buster's choice was to forego a rematch with Mike Tyson and decided to take on Evander Holyfield. Doing his homework, Holyfield witnessed the Douglas - Tyson match viewing Buster's style, strategy, and his very effective uppercut punch.

On October 25, 1990, at the Mirage Hotel in Las Vegas, the new Champ faced challenger, Evander Holyfield. Buster didn't look the same as eight months earlier. He was fifteen pounds heavier and without the appearance of his championship win. Therefore, Buster didn't perform as he did in his Tyson bout and resorted to his winning uppercut punches on Holyfield once too often. In the 3rd round, Buster let the uppercut go, and Holyfield was waiting for it. Holyfield avoided it and countered with a straight right, which ended Buster's short Championship reign. Holyfield gladly took Buster's titles to become the 33rd Undisputed World Heavyweight Champion. They both received over 24 million dollars, and Buster decided it was time to retire, while Holyfield felt that it was just the beginning for him.

In retirement, Buster's weight soared to 400 pounds, and at one point, he nearly died while in a diabetic coma. However, Buster, a true warrior, got back into shape and returned to the game. He won six straight bouts, including one in 1996 and 5 of them in 1997. He lost only one contest to Lou Savarese, but came back with two more wins by knockout, then retired for good.

Today, Buster lives near his hometown of Columbus, Ohio, and stays busy training other fighters in the gym. He was featured in some films and a video game. Buster earned 35 million dollars in his career and at last report, has a net worth of 15 million dollars.

MY OBSERVATION

Buster had Boxing in his blood, beginning with his father, who was a good Boxer that turned trainer. Buster was a big, strong man who possessed a very effective, reaching jab. He was supposed to be another stepping stone for Mike Tyson as a 42-1 underdog, but he was determined to take down the Champion. However, just eight months later, it appears that he lost sight of his goals or maybe underestimated Evander Holyfield. Buster handed over his title after one of the shortest reigns of a Heavyweight Champion. However, James "Buster" Douglas will always be remembered as the man who knocked out the invincible, "Iron" Mike Tyson!

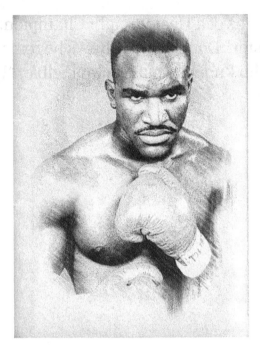

EVANDER HOLYFIELD

"The Real Deal"

B: Oct. 19, 1962
Born: Atmore, Alabama
6' 2" / 225 lbs.
Record: 44-10-2 29 KO's

Champion:
Oct. 25, 1990 - Nov. 13, 1992
Nov. 6, 1993 - Nov. 4, 1995
Nov. 9, 1996 - Nov. 13, 1999
Aug. 12, 2000 - Mar. 3, 2001

E vander Holyfield was a World Cruiserweight Champion and is the only man in history to own the prestigious title of being a "Four-Time World Champion Boxing Champion"! He is also in a select group that competed in the Light Heavyweight, Cruiserweight, and Heavyweight divisions.

Evander won a Boys Club tournament when he was seven, and by the time he was 15, he was considered an accomplished Boxer. He finished out his impressive amateur record of 160-14, with 76 Knockouts. Evander also won the National Golden Gloves Championship and a Bronze Medal in the 1984 Olympic games in Los Angeles.

Evander turned pro that same year and became known to the other contenders as a fighter who trained hard and was hard to handle in the ring. After just a couple of years as a pro and a dozen bouts, he took on Dwight Muhammad Qawi. Evander captured the WBA version of the Cruiserweight title in a Split Decision at the Omni Coliseum in Atlanta, Georgia. April 1988 pitted him against Carlos DeLeon and a chance at the Undisputed Cruiserweight title, and after an eighth-round Knockout, the title was his.

Evander knew a move up to the Heavyweight Division would undoubtedly yield a bigger payday and more fame. In July 1988, his 18th pro bout, he took on James "Quick" Tillis for his first heavyweight match up. This first pro contest ended in Evander's favor with a 5th round RTD decision, (opponent quit between rounds), for him. He was on his way, and after two more bouts, Evander met Michael Dokes for the WBC Continental Americas Heavyweight title. He stopped Dokes in the 10th round to win one version of the Heavyweight title. Evander defended this title three times and, then a big payday came when he got his chance at James "Buster" Douglas, who owned the Lineal and Undisputed Heavyweight title.

Douglas had just knocked out the invincible Mike Tyson in February 1990. Evander witnessed their bout and was aware of Douglas' favorite and effective uppercut punches that did Tyson in. On October 25, 1990, Evander was excited to get his shot at Douglas and his titles. When Douglas tried his trademark uppercuts on this night, Evander was ready. The third round proved to be just the right time to counter Buster's perfectly placed uppercut. As Buster let the deadly punch go, Evander countered with a straight right cross to shock Douglas, and after a barrage of punches, knocked him out. This exciting win for Evander made him the 33rd Lineal Heavyweight Champion of the World!

Evander, the new Champion, defended his title three times against former Champions, including "Big" George Foreman, Bert Cooper, and Larry "The "Easton Assassin" Holmes in Las Vegas. However, his string of wins was broken when he faced an always tough Riddick Bowe on November 13, 1992, in Las Vegas. He lost by a Unanimous Decision, but Evander wasn't the kind to give up. He came back in town to put away Alex Stewart in June of 1993, and on November

6, took back his title with a decision over Riddick Bowe. This win earned him the World Heavyweight Champion Crown for the second time. Evander then took on Michael Moorer for a WBO match in April of 1994. It was another setback as he lost by a Majority Decision to Moorer. Looking into the future, Evander took on his old nemesis, Riddick Bowe, once more on November 4, 1995, but suffered a TKO loss in the 8th round.

Evander came back once more to defeat a tough Bobby Czyz. He was then offered a big chance at "Iron" Mike Tyson on November 9, 1996, at the MGM Grand in Las Vegas. Evander stood his ground and traded punches with "Iron" Mike, and on this night proved to be too much for Tyson. Evander stunned the crowd as he stopped Mike in the 11th round. Evander took the WBA title and became a Heavyweight Champion title holder three times.

A little more than six months later, Evander gave Tyson a rematch and another chance at that title. It was another exciting, slugfest with plenty of toe to toe action. In a scheduled twelve round event, Tyson shockingly bit Evander's ear while in a clinch. Referee, Mills Lane halted the action and deducted two points from Tyson. To give Mike another chance and the fans more entertainment, Lane then let the bout continue. However, there was no lesson learned by Tyson as he unbelievably bit a part of Evander's ear entirely off! Mills Lane had no other choice but to disqualify Tyson and award the fiasco to Evander in the third round.

Mike's excuse was that Evander continuously head-butted in close in this fight as he had in their first matchup, without consequences.

Later in 1997, Evander won his IBF title bout against Michael Moorer in Las Vegas at the Thomas and Mack Center. Moving forward, Evander eliminated Vaughn Bean and was ready to take on "all-comers" defending his WBA title. Lennox Lewis stepped up next on March 13, 1999, in Madison Square Garden. This tough matchup was declared a "Draw" in which Evander retained his crown. However, with nothing settled in the first matchup, Evander met Lewis again eight months later at the Thomas and Mack Center in Las Vegas. This time, Lewis had the better night and took a twelve round Unanimous Decision for the WBA, IBF, WBC, IBO, and lineal title to become the 34th Undisputed World Heavyweight Champion.

Evander was not deterred and continued on his quest as he took on John Ruiz in a trilogy beginning on August 12, 2000. Evander won their first contest by a Unanimous Decision and recaptured the WBA vacant title and became the first man to win a World Heavyweight Championship for the fourth time! However, just months later, on March 3, 2001, during a rematch with Ruiz, he lost his title once more. He performed better in their "Rubber match" in 2001 when the decision was a "Draw," but Ruiz maintained the title.

In December 2002, Evander lost a Unanimous Decision to Chris Byrd and in 2004, also lost to James

Toney and Larry Donald. That same year he suffered a different loss, his Boxing license for failing a physical exam. However, he passed his next exam and regained his license in 2006.

Evander got right back to work, winning against Jeremy Bates and Fres Oquendo in 2006. Next, he took out Vinny Maddalone and Lou Savaraese, but lost to two Russians, Sultan Ibragimov and Nikolai Valuev. Evander got back on track and won with an eight-round TKO over Francois Botha in a "No Contest." He also won against Sherman Williams in the Bahamas, which was a WBF title win for Evander. For his grand finale, he met Brian Nielsen on May 5, 2011, in Copenhagen, Denmark. Evander won by TKO in the 10th round to go out on top as he then retired from competition. Evander will be remembered as a warrior who would never give up.

Evander has been considered and ranked by experts as one of the best in Boxing history in three weight divisions and categories. He continues to promote and further the world of Boxing around the country while his home base is Atlanta, Georgia. Reports indicate that Evander earned 250 million dollars in his career and now has a net worth of 500 thousand dollars.

MY OBSERVATION

Evander always had a pleasant disposition and was loved by fans and respected by his foes. He was a very determined Boxer who used various combinations to suit his opponent and win. He fought them all, journeymen, former Champions, and current Champions. A loss never deterred him as he would come right back again and again. He was a true warrior who continues to help young Boxers and Boxing Gyms everywhere. I loved watching his nonstop, creative combinations!

RIDDICK BOWE

B: Aug. 10, 1967
Born: Brooklyn, New York
6' 5" / 245 lbs.
Record: 43-1-1 33 KO's

Champion:
Nov. 13, 1992 - Nov. 6,1993

Riddick Lamont Bowe was number twelve of thirteen children who lived in the Brownsville neighborhood of Brooklyn, New York. Coincidentally, Riddick attended the same elementary school as another future World Champion, Mike Tyson. Actually, one more future Champion lived in the same neighborhood, Shannon Briggs. Michael Moorer was also born in Brooklyn which made these four men the second and only other city in the world to have four World Heavyweight Champions,... Louisville Kentucky is the first.

Riddick wisely looked for a future after Boxing by attending Kingsborough Community College, where he studied drama and business administration.

Boxing for Riddick began at the Bedford-Stuyvesant Gym as a teenager in New York. He started winning early on as he captured the New York Golden Gloves tournament at just seventeen-years-old. He won the 1985 and 1986, 178lb Championships, and the 1987 and 1988 Super Heavyweight Championships.

Riddick moved on to the 1988 Olympics in Seoul, Korea, meeting another future World Champion, Lennox Lewis. Riddick lost to Lewis and was awarded a Silver medal in the Super-Heavyweight division after losing this close and controversial bout. His impressive, amateur record was 104 wins to only 18 losses as he looked forward to a professional career.

Riddick turned pro in March 1989 and hired famous trainer, Eddie Futch who said Riddick was one of the most talented Boxers that he had ever seen. Together they took on thirteen journeymen that year and won every match by stoppage except for only one Unanimous Decision.

In 1991, Riddick took on tougher talent and defeated

some top contenders, including Tyrell Biggs, Tony Tubbs, and Bruce Seldon in the seven bouts for that year.

Riddick only had four bouts in 1992, but one of them was magic for him. On Friday, November 13, he took on lineal Champion, Evander Holyfield, at the Thomas and Mack Center in Las Vegas, Nevada. The Champion couldn't hold off the challenger, and Holyfield lost the 12 round Unanimous Decision to give Riddick the lineal and Undisputed WBA, WBC, and IBF Heavyweight crowns.

The new Champion's first title defense was against veteran Michael Dokes on February 6, 1993, in Madison Square Garden. Riddick's string of wins continued with a first-round TKO over Dokes to retain his newly won titles. Jesse Ferguson fell next in Washington DC on May 22 by a 2nd round KO before Riddick met Evander Holyfield for the second time. The only loss of his professional career came a year after winning the titles. On Saturday, November 6, 1993, Riddick came in twenty pounds overweight in a Caesars Palace outdoor event in Las Vegas. There was also an unusual prank that stopped the momentum of the bout for a half-hour. James' Fan Man' Miller parachuted into the ring from out of nowhere and was arrested. This spectacle could have had an added effect on either Boxer that night. Riddick did lose this night by a Majority Decision, meaning two judges awarded Holyfield the Decision, and one judge called the match a Draw... Riddick wasn't discouraged!

Riddick had only two bouts in 1994, a "No Contest" with Buster Mathis, then a 12 round Unanimous Decision over Larry Donald. Caesars Palace hosted the Donald bout on December 3, for the WBC Continental Americas Heavyweight title. Now, back on track, Riddick took on Brit Herbie Hide on March 11, 1995. After six knockdowns, Riddick KO'd Hide in the 6th round at the MGM Grand in Las Vegas to win the relatively new WBO title belt.

Riddick defended his new crown against tough, Jorge Luis Gonzalez with a KO on June 17, 1995, at the MGM in Vegas. He then prepared for his rubber match (third bout), with former Champion, Evander Holyfield. They met again at Caesars Palace on Saturday, November 6, 1995. Riddick KO'd Holyfield and became the only man to do so in his fifty-seven fights.

Moving on, Riddick had only two bouts in 1996, both against the same strong competitor, Andrew Golota. Golota seemed to be doing well in their first bout, but kept hitting below the belt and was eventually disqualified in the 9th round for low blows. With this decision, mayhem broke out in Madison Square Garden, as it seemed everyone around the ring was pushing, shoving, and throwing punches. However, after several minutes of chaos, the decision still stood. A rematch was scheduled in the Convention Hall in Atlantic City, New Jersey, for the two warriors. Golota looked strong this time also, but his low blows continued until another 9th round Disqualification loss was handed to him.

Riddick dropped out of the Boxing game for almost eight years, but came back for three more bouts. He won a TKO in 2004 over Marcus Rhode and a Split Decision over Billy Zumbrun on April 7, 2005. He added a Unanimous Decision over Gene Pukall in Mannheim, Germany on December 13, 2008, to end his competitive career.

Riddick had a very high percentage of wins, as 75% were TKO or KO's. He was never stopped by TKO or KO'd himself, and his only loss was a Majority Decision to Evander Holyfield. Actually, there were only three other Heavyweight Boxers in history that are in this group, Gene Tunney, Rocky Marciano, and Nikolai Valuev. In addition, to his credit, Riddick was also the only man to TKO the four-time Heavyweight Champion, Evander Holyfield.

The Ring Magazine ranks Riddick as the 32nd best Heavyweight Champion of all time, and he was inducted into The International Hall of Fame in 2015. Riddick Bowe resides in Fort Washington, Maryland.

MY OBSERVATION

Riddick Bowe is well deserving to be included in the top sector of Heavyweight Champions. He won several titles as an amateur and only lost one amateur title bout to the Olympic Gold Medal winner, Lennox Lewis. Riddick never got to avenge this loss in his pro career. He only had one bad night as a pro when he lost a bout to the four-time Heavyweight Champion Evander Holyfield by Majority Decision. However, Riddick avenged Holyfield two other times, one Unanimous Decision and one TKO... Riddick is the only man to stop Holyfield! I liked Riddick's smooth and powerful style.

MICHAEL MOORER

B: Nov. 12, 1967
B: Brooklyn, New York
6'2" / 215 lbs.
Record: 52-4-1

Champion:
Apr. 22, 1994 - Nov. 5, 1994

M ichael Lee Moorer was the third of four World Heavyweight Champions born in Brooklyn, New York. Brooklyn is the second and only other city in the world that boasts four World Heavyweight Champions.

Louisville, Kentucky is first and the other with Marvin Hart, Muhammad Ali, Jimmy Ellis, and Greg Page. However, Michael didn't stay in Brooklyn; he moved to Monessen, Pennsylvania, as a youngster.

Michael began his life in sports by playing football in elementary school and starred on his high school team. Michael's grandfather was a former New York Golden Gloves Champion, and when Michael was age eleven, his grandfather believed that Michael would benefit from lessons that Boxing offers.

Michael quickly took to Boxing and developed into a good amateur. To further his skills, he moved to Detroit, Michigan, to join veteran trainer Emanuel Steward at his famed Kronk Gym. Michael quickly developed as he won the Light Middleweight Championship in 1986 and amassed an amateur record of 48 wins and 16 losses.

Michael turned pro in 1988 in the Light Heavyweight division and won eleven bouts by knockout. This included the WBO Light Heavyweight Championship over Ramzi Hassan of Jordan. The new Champion defended his title nine times in 1989 and 1990 before moving up to the Heavyweight division in 1991.

Michael met veteran Bert Cooper at the Etess Arena in Atlantic City, New Jersey, on May 15, 1992, for the vacant WBO Heavyweight title. Michael finally won this tough match by a TKO to become one of the big four divisional World Heavyweight Champions.

Michael switched trainers and defended his WBO crown six times, then challenged lineal Champion,

Evander Holyfield, for his WBA and IBF titles. This match took place at Caesar's Palace in Las Vegas, Nevada, on Friday, April 22, 1994. Holyfield dropped Michael in the second round, but he pulled himself up and rallied to a Majority Decision. Michael became the first southpaw lineal Heavyweight Boxing Champion in history!

Seven months later, former 1973 Heavyweight Champion, "Big George" Foreman challenged undefeated Michael for his titles. They met at the MGM Grand in Las Vegas on Saturday, November 5, 1994. As the bout progressed, young Michael moved and traded punches with Foreman for nine rounds. However, Michael was eventually caught with a flurry in the 10th round to lose his lineal belts and suffer the first knockout of his professional career.

Moving on, Michael won his next four bouts, which included the vacant IBF title over Axel Schultz in his home country of Germany on June 22, 1996, by a Split Decision.

A rematch of Evander Holyfield took place on November 8, 1997, at the Thomas and Mack Center in Las Vegas. The WBA title was up for grabs, and Michael put his IBF title on the block also. The outcome was different this time, as Michael was knocked down five times before the doctor stopped the fight in the eighth round. The always tough Holyfield collected the two titles as Michael picked up his second defeat of his pro career.

Michael retired for three years, but came back

to competition on November 17, 2000. He had four wins and only one Draw that took place against Dale Crowe at the Soaring Eagle Casino in Mount Pleasant, Michigan on July 27, 2001. Michael's only third career loss came by a first-round knockout to veteran Boxer, David Tua, at the Etess Center in Atlantic City on August 17, 2002.

Michael had a variety of decisions in his last ten bouts, with only one more loss to Eliseo Castillo of Cuba in Miami, Florida, on July 3, 2004. Michael then met Vassiliy Jirov of Kazakhstan and won by TKO in the ninth round to capture the WBA-NABA and WBC Continental Americas Heavyweight titles. Michael earned the status of handing Jirov the first knockout of his career. Michael had six more wins before retiring in 2008.

Michael had the privilege of working with four of the best trainers Boxing history. Emanuel Steward, Georgie Benton, Teddy Atlas, and Freddie Roach all helped shape Michael's winning career.

MY OBSERVATION

Michael was a Light Heavyweight who beefed up to the Heavyweight division. This could have been a disadvantage as he was competing with many men that were quite a bit bigger than him. I loved his slick style, which showed his offense and defensive talents. His Southpaw stance could also make it awkward for both Boxers. He had a good amateur record and won titles in his amateur and professional career, including the lineal Championship. He only had four losses to bigger men in his pro career. Michael was a great Champion in several weight divisions.

SHANNON BRIGGS

B: Dec. 4, 1971
Born: Brooklyn, New York
6' 4" / 245 lbs.
Record: 60-6-1 53 KO's
"Over 50 KO Club"

Champion:
Nov. 22,1997 - Mar. 28, 1998

Coincidentally, Shannon Briggs became the third World Heavyweight Champion from the same neighborhood of Brownsville and the fourth from the city of Brooklyn, New York. Mike Tyson, Riddick Bowe, and Michael Moorer all preceded Shannon for the Heavyweight Crown. Shannon said that he was impressed by seeing Mike Tyson in the neighborhood, which greatly gave him the motivation to begin Boxing.

Shannon joined O'Pharrow's Starrett City Boxing Club in Brooklyn at age seventeen in 1989 and quickly developed into a good student. In 1991 he became the New York City Golden Gloves Heavyweight Champion, the New York State Heavyweight Champion, and the PAL (Police Athletic League) National Heavyweight Champion. In 1992, Shannon also became the US Amateur Heavyweight Champion.

In 1992, Shannon turned pro and added veteran trainer, Teddy Atlas to his team. Incredibly, he won his first twenty-five bouts, with the majority of them being TKO and KO's. However, he was surprised when he took on journeyman, Darroll Wilson in Atlantic City on March 15, 1996. This unbelievable off night was his first loss by a third-round KO that broke his professional winning streak.

Shannon had one more winning bout in 1996 against Louisvillian, Tim Ray, and four more victories in 1997, including current World Champion, George Foreman. He met Foreman in the Etess Arena in Atlantic City, New Jersey, on Saturday, November 22. Shannon fought a defensive boxing match staying away from Foreman's power, but did suffer a battering and a broken nose. However, Shannon was able to pull off the win with a Majority Decision as he took the lineal Heavyweight Crown from "Big" George Foreman.

Shannon met contender Lennox Lewis for his next bout and was his first title defense at the Boardwalk Convention Center. It was just three months later on Sunday, March 8, 1998. After three knockdowns, the referee stopped the fight in the fifth round to give Lewis the TKO win. This loss gave Lewis the lineal Heavyweight Championship of the World after Shannon's only three and a half months reign.

After the loss to Lennox Lewis in 1998, Shannon only lost four bouts. Two of them were to great talent, Sedrick Fields, and Jameel McCline, and two were top-ranked contenders, Sultan Ibragimov and Vatali Klitschko.

Ibragimov met Shannon at the Boardwalk Hall in Atlantic City on June 2, 2007 and put up his WBO title that he had won from Siarhei Liakhovich on November 4, 2006. Shannon lost by a 12 round Unanimous Decision as he naturally didn't perform well after suffering pneumonia just two months earlier.

Four bouts later, on October 16, 2010, Shannon met Vatali Klitschko in search of his WBO title. Shannon survived the 12 rounds, but lost another Unanimous Decision at the O2 World Arena in Hamburg, Germany.

Shannon won his last nine bouts by KO except only one by Unanimous Decision over Raphael Zumbano Love at Remington Park in Oklahoma City, Oklahoma. This match had Shannon capturing the vacant WBA-NABA Heavyweight title. His very next bout earned him the NABA World Boxing Council Latino title over Cory Phelps in Winston-Salem, North Carolina.

Shannon retired from Boxing competition after his last bout with a first-round KO over Emilio Ezequiel in London, England, on May 21, 2016... he retired as a Champion with his titles.

Shannon became involved in acting as he played parts on TV, movies, and was featured in some videos. He resides in his hometown of Brooklyn, New York.

MY OBSERVATION

Shannon was a strong Heavyweight who fought the best around. He captured several title belts, including the lineal Championship, which makes him among the best. He had a winning amateur career, professional career, and went out as a Champion which impresses me.

LENNOX LEWIS

B: Sept. 2, 1965
Born: London, England
6'5" / 245 lbs.
Record: 41-2 32 KO's

Champion:
Mar. 28, 1998 - Apr. 22, 2001
Nov. 17, 2001 - Retirement

Lennox Claudius Lewis was born to Jamaican parents who lived in London, England, in September 1965. The family moved to Ontario,

Canada, when Lennox was a youngster of just twelve years old. He played football, soccer, and basketball in school and helped his team win the AAA Ontario Basketball Championship.

The Basketball Champion took up Boxing in 1978 and loved it. Lennox progressed quickly and won an amateur Gold medal in 1983 and represented Canada in the 1984 Olympics, but lost in the quarter-finals. He was very disappointed and decided to remain an amateur in order to compete in the 1988 Olympics in Seoul, Korea. It was worth the wait as he did win a Gold Medal in the Super Heavyweight Division for Canada over American, Riddick Bowe. Incidentally, Lennox was the seventh Gold Medal Champion to become a professional World Heavyweight Champion. Floyd Patterson, Muhammad Ali, Joe Frazier, George Foreman, Leon Spinks, and Michael Spinks were the other six at this time. Lennox finished his amateur career with a winning 85-9 record.

Lennox moved back to England, turned pro and won his first bout, in the first round at The Royal Albert Hall in London on June 27, 1989. He actually won his first thirty-five bouts, all nearly by knockout, over the best opponents in the game. He won his first title, The European Heavyweight Crown, on just his fourteenth bout over Jean-Maurice Chanet on October 31, 1990. Lennox piled up the Championship belts as he won the British Heavyweight title over undefeated Brit Gary Mason four months later, and the Commonwealth Heavyweight title over Derel

Williams on his twenty-first outing. This matchup took place at Wembley Arena in London on April 30, 1992. All three of these titles were won in the first three years as a professional!

On October 31, 1992, one year after winning the European title, Lennox KO'd Razor Ruddock in the 2nd round to become the number one contender to the WBC throne. After this win, Champion Riddick Bowe dumped his WBC title belt into the trash can rather than fight Lennox. This incident forced the WBC to award Lennox the Championship on December 14, 1992. Incidentally, there was only one other Heavyweight Champion crowned without a Boxing contest, Kenny Norton. The WBC acknowledged Kenny Norton as the Champion in 1978 after Spinks signed to a rematch with Ali.

Lennox defended his crown three times, including a Unanimous Decision over Tony Tucker, then took on another Brit, Frank Bruno, on October 1, 1993. The Champ TKO'd Bruno in the 7th round in Cardiff Arms Park, Cardiff, Wales to soundly confirm his WBC Heavyweight title.

Lennox defended with a TKO against Phil Jackson at the Boardwalk Convention Center in Atlantic City on May 6, 1994, before taking on Oliver McCall at the Wembley Arena in London on September 24, 1994. Lennox was undefeated with twenty-five victories and was at home in the Wembley Arena in London. It was a shocking second-round TKO loss for Lennox that stunned him and the fans. He lost the WBC title, which made him reassess things, including his team. Lennox then hired veteran trainer Emanuel Steward out of Detroit, Michigan, a coach of many other World Champions including, Wladimir Klitschko and Tyson Fury.

Lennox began with his new team and produced three TKO wins, including a beatdown of Tommy Morison at Convention Hall in Atlantic City, winning the WBC Heavyweight title. Ray Mercer fell by Majority Decision before a February 7, 1997 rematch with Oliver McCall, for the WBC title held at the Las Vegas Hilton. This was a very strange meeting as McCall lost the first three rounds and just refused to fight in the next two. McCall totally stopped fighting and had some sort of emotional breakdown, so the referee had to declare the bout a TKO win for Lennox.

Two more victories, a Disqualification win over Henry Akinwande, and a first-round KO over Andrew Golota brought Lennox to a matchup against the lineal Champion, Shannon Briggs, on Friday, March 20, 1998, at the Boardwalk Hall in Atlantic City, New Jersey. It was a short night as Lennox won a TKO halfway through the fifth round. Lennox retained his WBC title and became the next lineal Heavyweight Champion of the World. A Brit hadn't won the World lineal Championship since Bob Fitzsimmons in 1897.

Lennox defended his title with a Unanimous Decision over Zeljko Mavrovic at the Mohegan Sun Casino. He then challenged Evander Holyfield for his WBA and IBF titles at Madison Square Garden in

New York on March 13, 1998. The bout was declared a Draw, which was subject to much controversy. Lennox retained his titles, and Holyfield retained his.

With nothing settled in March, a rematch was scheduled for Friday, November 13, 1998, at the Thomas and Mack Center in Las Vegas. This time the contest also included the vacant IBO title. Lennox was victorious this time with a Unanimous Decision and the Undisputed Heavyweight Championship of the World.

Lennox defended his title three times against Michael Grant, Frans Botha, and David Tua, winning by KO, TKO, and Unanimous Decision. Hasim Rahman, a 15-1 underdog, challenged Lennox in Carnival City, Brakpan, South Africa, on Sunday, April 22, 2001. Rahman surprised Lennox with an overhand right that KO'd him in the 5th round. This greatly shocked the Boxing fans as Rahman became the new lineal and Undisputed World Heavyweight Champion.

Seven months later, on Saturday, November 17, the Rahman rematch was on at Mandalay Bay Resort in Las Vegas. There were no surprises this time as Lennox was more careful and ultimately pounded Rahman until he knocked him out in the 4th round. This win made Lennox a two-time lineal World Champion. Until now, there are only five Champions who regained the lineal title, Floyd Patterson, Muhammad Ali, Evander Holyfield, George Foreman, and Lennox.

The much-anticipated bout against Mike Tyson was on at the Pyramid in Memphis, Tennessee, on June 8,

2002. Mike was looking for his title back, but it was not to be. Lennox kept the brawling Tyson away with jabs until Lennox hit Tyson with a right cross to KO "Iron" Mike and retain his World Championship belts. It was a high grossing deal, with both each earning 17.5 million dollars.

Lennox had one last title defense against the WBC number one challenger, Vatali Klitschko, that took place at the Staples Center in Los Angeles on June 21, 2003. Lennox got busy and landed shots until one cut Klitschko's eye. This cut actually ended the fight for a TKO win for Lennox. Lennox earned seven million dollars, and Klitschko earned 1.4 million for this contest.

Lennox is one of only four Heavyweights to end his career as Champion with a world title fight victory. He is one of only three Champions to have beaten every opponent that he faced, at one time or another, during his career. Ingemar Johannsson and Rocky Marciano are the other two. He is considered as one of the best Heavyweights and was named "Fighter of the Year" in 1999 by the Boxing Writers Association of America.

Lennox was inducted into the 2008 Canadian sports Hall of Fame, 2009 International Hall of Fame, and the 2012 Ontario, Canada Hall of Fame. In 2018 the Boxing News ranked him as the third-best Heavyweight Champion of all time behind Muhammad Ali and Joe Louis.

Lennox has been featured on TV, in movies, in videos, and has been an HBO Boxing commentator. He resides in both Miami, Florida, and Jamaica.

MY OBSERVATION

Lennox had a very reserved and formal personality. His boxing style was a very methodical machine. He was an effective puncher who would mix it up if necessary. He beat every opponent that he faced at some point in his career. Lennox represented Canada and Great Britain well and is one of my all-time favorite personalities and Boxers.

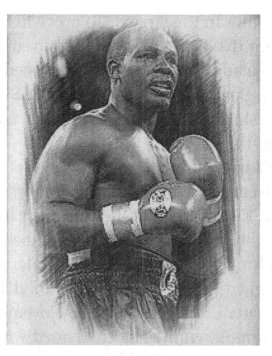

HASIM RAHMAN

B: Nov.7, 1972
B: Baltimore, Maryland
6'2" / 240 lbs.
Record: 50-9-2 40 KO's

Champion:
Apr. 22, 2001 - Nov. 17, 2001

Hasim Sharif Rahman was a very tough guy who grew up in the East Coast city of Baltimore, Maryland. He may have interacted occasionally with the wrong crowd and actually did get shot several different times in the streets. To prove his resilience, he was shot five times once and survived. That kind of tenacity made him a force to be reckoned with after he took up Boxing at the age of twenty. Since he got such a late start, he turned pro after only ten amateur bouts in 1994.

Hasim's natural talent and power was evident as he won twenty-four of his first twenty-nine outings by TKO or KO. In the mix, he won the vacant USBA Heavyweight Belt over Jeff Wooden in Rochester, New York on July 15, 1997. He added the IBF Intercontinental Heavyweight title over Obed Sullivan at the famed Apollo Theater in New York City on November 1, 1997.

The Champ's winning streak ended when he met the always tenacious David Tua from New Zealand in Miami, Florida, on December 12, 1998. Hasim outboxed Tua and seemed to be on his way to another victory when one of Tua's explosive punches caught him after the 9th round bell. Instead of a Disqualification, the referee let the bout continue. Tua took advantage of this mistake and proceeded to pound Hasim, who was still stunned. So, the referee stopped the contest and awarded a TKO win to Tua in the 10th round. Tua also collected Hasim's IBF and USBA title belts.

Hasim moved on and picked up a couple more wins, a 5th round TKO over Michael Rush in New York City and a 1st round KO over Arthur Weathers in Miami, Florida.

Next on the agenda was Oleg Maskaev from Uzbekistan. Maskaev had only two losses in nineteen bouts to two very tough competitors, Oliver McCall and David Tua. Maskaev was ready this night on November 6, 1999, at the Boardwalk, in New Jersey. However, Hasim wasn't prepared as he admittedly took Maskaev lightly. However, Hasim did well into the 8th round until Maskaev took advantage and won by Knockout.

Moving on, Hasim's very next bout was five months later on March 1, 2000. It was for the Maryland State Heavyweight Championship title against Marion Wilson in Woodlawn, Maryland. Hasim won that title and added another win to his resume as he won by a Unanimous Decision over South African, Corrie Sanders. It took place at Bally's Park Place in Atlantic City, New Jersey, on May 20, 2000. Hasim TKO'd Sanders in the 7th round to win the bout and add the WBU Heavyweight belt to his trophy case. Next, Frankie Swindell fell by an RTD a couple of months later, which put him in line for a shot at the lineal Champion, Lennox Lewis.

Hasim was a 20 to 1 underdog as he flew down to Brakpan, South Africa, for the Sunday, April 22, 2001 match up. It was a slugfest from the start that had both men landing bombs for four rounds. Like a guided missile, Hasim threw a huge overhand right as Lennox was moving down the ropes. The punch exploded onto Lewis' head to KO him near the end of the 5th round. Hasim ended Lewis' year and half reign and brought the lineal Heavyweight Championship back to the United States.

Lewis legally forced Hasim to abide by the contract that requires an immediate rematch. This return matchup took place on Saturday, November 17, 2001, at the Mandalay Bay Resort in Las Vegas. Lewis wanted his titles back and was ready this time. Lennox was on guard this time and was looking for payback. Shots were exchanged until Lewis put the one-two combination together to end the show in the 4th round. Lewis regained his lineal titles and became the fifth, two-time World Heavyweight Champion. Lewis earned eleven million dollars, and Hasim earned ten million.

Hasim had four disappointments after losing the title to Lewis. He met his only challenge in 2002 on June 21 against the ultimate puncher, Evander Holyfield. Punches were traded until there was a clash of heads in the 8th round. This impact caused a giant hematoma to the left side of Hasim's head. This dangerous situation caused the doctor to stop the bout as Hasim was very disappointed. The accidental headbutt impaired Hasim to continue, which gave Holyfield the win in the Boardwalk Hall in Atlantic City.

A rematch with David Tua ended in a Draw in March 2003, and a Unanimous Decision loss to John Ruiz in December closed that year of bad luck.

2004 saw five bouts and five wins for Hasim as he won by two KO's, one TKO, and two Unanimous Decisions. There was only one contest in 2005 for him against Monte Barrett at the United Center in Chicago.

However, this was a big win as he collected the Interim World Boxing Council Heavyweight title.

Only two bouts in 2006 for the new WBC Interim Champion. The first was against the very defensive, James Toney who challenged Hasim for the WBC title. They met at the Boardwalk Hall in Atlantic City. The bout was declared a Draw in which Hasim retained the title. On August 12 Hasim took on Oleg Maskaev from Uzbekistan at the Thomas and Mack Center in Las Vegas to battle for the WBC Heavyweight title. Maskaev owned the night with a twelve round TKO over Hasim to take the title.

Hasim marched right back with three TKO's and a Unanimous Decision in 2007. He took the Interim NABF title over Taurus Sykes and the NABF title over Zuri Lawrence on November 15 that year. On July 16, 2008, a rematch with James Toney was set for the WBO Heavyweight title belt. They exchanged blows until the doctor stopped the affair due to another accidental headbutt to Hasim's left eye in the third round. It was ruled a "No Contest" in which neither man won. The rules are, in case of an accidental headbutt in the first four rounds, no one wins. After the fourth round, they can go to the scorecards.

Hasim got another chance at the big prize against Wladimir Klitschko on December 13, 2008, in Mannheim, Germany. His goal was the WBO, IBO, and the IBF titles. However, it was another setback as he lost by a 7th round TKO to Klitschko. Hasim would not get another title shot for the next two and a half years.

Hasim didn't get discouraged or quit. He won his next five bouts in the next four years, all by TKO and KO's. He got one last shot at a title on September 29, 2012. It was for the WBA World Heavyweight belt. He was almost thirty years old and a number one contender when he met Alexander Povetkin in Hamburg, Germany. This was the beginning of the end of Hasim's career as he lost by a second-round TKO.

Almost two years later, he had one last attempt as he met club fighter Anthony Nansen in Auckland, New Zealand. Hasim was very disappointed as he lost a Unanimous Decision to close out his Boxing career with retirement.

Hasim Rahman now resides happily in his hometown of Baltimore, Maryland.

MY OBSERVATION

Hasim was born a warrior. When he was on, he was very impressive. He could punch in bunches and from all angles. However, sometimes, he elected to fight off the ropes, and that never works too well. He was on the night that he landed his big overhand to KO Lennox Lewis and take the lineal Heavyweight Crown. Hasim was a well-deserved competitor and Champion.

WLADIMIR KLITSCHKO

B: March 25, 1976
B: Semey, Kazakhstan
6'6" / 250 lbs.
Record: 64-5-0 53 KO's
"Over 50 KO Club"

Champion:
Jun. 20, 2009 - Nov. 28, 2015

Wladimir Klitschko is in a unique club with his brother, Vatali. They are the second brother duo to win a World Heavyweight Championship title. They are also the only brothers in history to be Heavyweight Champions at the same time. Wladimir reigned as the WBA Super Heavyweight, IBF, WBO, "The Ring," and lineal Champion, and Vatali owned the WBC title at the same time. They never fought each other for the lineal title as a promise to their Mother.

Wladimir was born in Semey, Kazakhstan (previously part of the Soviet Union). He began his amateur career in the late 1980s and was very successful as he won several titles and championships. Wladimir also won the gold medal in Boxing in the Super-Heavyweight division at the 1996 Summer Olympics in Atlantic, Georgia. He then ended his amateur career with an impressive 134-6 record.

Wladimir turned pro on November 16, 1996, with a first-round KO over Mexico's Fabian Meza in Hamburg, Germany. Incidentally, most of Wladimir's bouts were in Germany as he had a strong connection there. His father was a Major General in the Soviet Army who was stationed there as part of his service.

Wladimir won most of his pro bouts by TKO or KO's, including his first WBC International contest on his seventeenth outing in Stuttgart, Germany. It was a KO in the 3rd round over American Marcus Mcintyre on Valentine's Day in 1998. He later defended this title seven times in 1998 before meeting American Ross Puritty in Kiev, Ukraine. This is when his luck when south as he lost his first match and the WBC title on December 8, 1998.

However, Wladimir got back on schedule of KO's

meeting Joseph Chingangu of Zambia and took the vacant WBA Intercontinental Heavyweight title belt. Chingangu retired in the corner after the 4ᵗʰ round on July 17, 1999. In his very next bout, the Champ picked up the vacant European Heavyweight title over German Axel Schulz with an 8ᵗʰ round TKO in Cologne, Germany.

A couple more KO's over American Phil Jackson and Hungarian Lajos Eros brought Wladimir over to Hanover, Germany to face Paea Wolfgramm of Tonga. This matchup was for the WBC Intercontinental and European Heavyweight titles on March 18, 2000. Wolfgramm only lasted two rounds of Wladimir's bombardment to watch the vacant title slip away.

Wladimir took on five Americans winning four by TKO and one by Unanimous Decision over a very elusive, Chris Byrd in Cologne, Germany, on October 14, 2000. The Champ added four more TKO's including veterans Ray Mercer and Jameel McCline. Next up was South African Corrie Sanders in Hanover, Germany. In a stunning upset, Sanders fiercely attacked Wladimir until he landed an overhand bomb to TKO Wladimir and take his WBO title. This was another major upset in Boxing history!

Wladimir won two more, but lost his third pro bout to Lamon Brewster at Mandalay Bay in April 2004. However, Wladimir didn't lose another match for over eleven years. As Wladimir got back on track, he had big wins, including a 7 round TKO over former Champion Hasim Rahman. He then won the vacant WBA

Intercontinental title, WBC-NABF, WBO-NABO, IBF, IBO, WBO Heavyweight titles before meeting Ruslan Chagaev of Uzbekistan. They both were in search of the vacant "The Ring" and the lineal World Heavyweight titles that were left open by retired Champion, Lennox Lewis. Chagaev just couldn't handle Wladimir and gave up at round nine to make Wladimir the new lineal Heavyweight Champion of the World. The contest took place in Gelsenkirchen, Germany, on Saturday, June 20, 2009, and was his 53rd pro bout.

Wladimir defended his titles eleven times in over six years before his last two bouts with future Champions Anthony Joshua and Tyson Fury, both of Great Britain. The Tyson Fury meeting took place at the Merkur Spiel Arena in Dusseldorf, Germany, on Saturday, November 28, 2015. This Unanimous Decision loss was evident that his career was winding down as Fury took the lineal World Championship from the long-time Champion Wladimir Klitschko.

Forty-one year old, Wladimir took some time off before one last outing against the underdog, Anthony Joshua at Wembley Stadium in London, England, on April 29, 2017. Both men traded punches with Wladimir hitting the canvas in round five and Joshua going down in round six. The back and forth continued until Wladimir went down twice in the eleventh after much Joshua punishment. The referee stepped in to stop the fight as the eleventh round closed. The bout ended as a TKO and the career of Wladimir Klitschko. Now, Anthony Joshua had just become aligned to meet the now lineal World Heavyweight Champion of the World, Tyson Fury. In August 2017, Wladimir retired from Boxing instead of seeking a rematch with Joshua.

Wladimir is deemed to be one of the hardest-hitting Heavyweights and considered by experts to be one of the best Heavyweights of all time. He took out twelve unbeaten Heavyweights and had the second most successful title defenses at 23, behind Joe Louis at 25. Larry Holmes had 20, and Muhammad Ali had 19.

Wladimir has been seen on TV, in movies, and makes personal appearances occasionally. He and brother, Vatali, are highly educated individuals that have doctorates in Sports Science. They also are the only other brothers to both have owned the World Heavyweight titles, Spinks brothers are the other two. The Klitschko's are the only brothers to hold the World Heavyweight titles at the same time. Wladimir and Vatali held all World Heavyweight titles for two and a half years from July 2011 to December 2013.

A special act was bestowed upon the brothers with a national postage stamp in their home country of Ukraine in 2010. A "far out" honor, was given to them as the Asteroid #212723 was named Klitschko for their achievements in 2007.

Vatali, the 6'7" younger brother, also practiced Karate, Kickboxing, and started his own successful Boxing career at the same time as Wladimir. They trained together and were on many of the same Boxing cards together. Vatali's amateur career ended with 195 wins to only 15 losses. His professional career summed up with 45 wins and only two losses, but there were no KO's, or Decisions against him. He only lost to Chris Byrd when he pulled a shoulder rotator cuff muscle during the bout and to Lennox Lewis when the referee stopped the bout due to a huge cut over his eye. Actually, he was ahead on the judges' score cards on both bouts when the contests were stopped. Amazingly, all of his wins were KO's except for four Unanimous Decisions.

Wladimir, the lineal Heavyweight Champion, and Vatali the WBC Heavyweight Champion never fought each other for the lineal title. They promised their mother to never compete against each other. However, in honor of the both of them, 2004 to 2015 became known as the Klitschko Era.

Vatali retired as the WBC Champion in 2013 to pursue politics and won the Mayor's race of Kiev, Ukraine, in 2014. He also became the leader of his political party in the very next year, in 2015.

It's unlikely that we'll ever see two brothers that are Heavyweight Boxing Champions at the same time again!

MY OBSERVATION

The "Klitschko Era" denotes the period when Wladimir and brother Vatali dominated the Boxing scene for over ten years. Wladimir was a very robotic and methodical fighter who was very powerful and usually had the reach advantage. Veteran trainer

Emanuel Steward was very instrumental in helping him capitalize on his advantages. Steward directed Wladimir to simply jab and move, then at the perfect moment, explode his right cross. It was a very simple but effective system. He held several titles, including the lineal Heavyweight Crown, for six and a half years. It is the longest reign second only to the immortal Joe Louis!

TYSON FURY

B: Aug. 12, 1988
B: Manchester, England
6'9" / 260 lbs.
Record: 29-0-1 20 KO's

Champion:
Nov. 28, 2015 - Present

Tyson Luke Fury was born to Irish parents, John and Amber Fury in England. Tyson grew up to become one of the largest Heavyweight Champions of all time. Unbelievably, he only weighed one pound at a premature birth in 1988. Immediately after birth, Tyson was fighting for his life, which motivated his father to name him after the great fighter, Mike Tyson, who was the World Champion at that time. It was a miracle that he survived, and it seems that Mike Tyson was a good omen for the young infant.

Many of Tyson's family were Boxers, including his father, brothers, and cousins. His father was also a bare-knuckle fighter like John L. Sullivan and the days before the Marquess of Queensbury rules.

Tyson quit school at age eleven and worked with his family at paving roads. Also, at the early age of ten, Tyson began boxing with his father as the trainer and as an amateur, represented Ireland and England. Later, Tyson boxed out of the Holy Family Boxing Club in Belfast, Ireland, and the Smithboro Boxing Club, where he won every bout in 2007.

Tyson won the AIBA Youth World Boxing Championship in 2006, the EU Junior Championship, and a Silver medal at the European Junior Championships in 2007. He also took the ABA Super weight title and ended his amateur career with 31 wins and only four losses, 26 by KO's.

Tyson turned pro in December 2008 and garnered a first-round TKO over Bela Gyongyosi of Hungary in Nottingham, England. Incidentally, his first seven bouts were by TKO or KO. On his eighth bout, he won a Decision over John McDermott in Brentwood, England, to capture the English Heavyweight title on September 11, 2009.

On Tyson's fifteenth matchup, he met undefeated Dersck Chisora in the Wembley Arena for the British and Commonwealth Heavyweight titles. On July 23, 2011, he took the title from Chisora by a Unanimous Decision. Only nine months later, Tyson met Martin Rogan at the Odyssey Arena in Belfast, Northern Ireland, for the vacant Irish Heavyweight title. Rogan couldn't take Tyson's punishment and fell by a TKO in the 5th round. Tyson became the new Irish Heavyweight Champion.

The Champ's very next bout was against American Vinny Maddalone for the vacant WBO Intercontinental Heavyweight title in Clevedon, England. Tyson TKO'd Maddalone in the 5th round to add this WBO title to his assortment. He took on three more Americans, winning all to eventually meet Dereck Chisora in a rematch. It took place on November 14, 2014, at the Excel in London, England. The prize was the European, WBO International, and the British Heavyweight titles. Chisora retired in the corner at the 10th round to hand Tyson the titles.

Wladimir Klitschko was next on the horizon at the Esprit Arena in Dusseldorf, Germany, on Saturday, November 28, 2015, for the WBA Super Heavyweight, IBF, IBO, WBO, "The Ring," and the lineal Championship. The 24-0 Tyson underdog won an unexciting bout by Unanimous Decision to become the new lineal Heavyweight Champion of the World!

Many problems immediately surfaced for Tyson. He lost his IBF title just ten days later because he had a rematch clause with Klitschko, which eliminated him from meeting their number one contender in their IBF organization.

Many other problems surfaced for Tyson, which caused a two-year hiatus. Contracts, drug tests, public statements, emotional problems, licensing, and more eventually robbed him of his current, stunning career. The anticipated Klitschko rematch never materialized.

On June 9, 2018, Tyson returned to the ring against Sefer Seferi of Albania in Manchester, England. Seferi proved to be little opposition as Tyson retired him at the 4th round. Francesco Pianeta of Italy fell next by Decision in Belfast, North Ireland, before Tyson met Deontay Wilder for the WBC title. After twelve rounds of back and forth, the bout was declared a Draw at the Staples Center in Los Angeles, California. Tyson landed more punches, but Wilder dropped Tyson twice with two quick knockdowns. Tyson maintained his lineal title, and Deontay saved his WBC title. Boxing fans looked forward to a rematch with these two warriors. This first contest was a PPV success, and promoters were looking for a bigger payday with the rematch.

After the Wilder fight, Tyson signed a five year, 100 million dollar contract with ESPN and Top Rank to make him comfortable for life.

Six months later, Tyson met 10 to 1 underdog Tom Schwarz of Germany at the MGM in Las Vegas on June 15, 2019, for the WBO Intercontinental Heavyweight title. Tyson dominated and made a short night of

Schwarz to win a second-round TKO to take Schwarz's title belt.

Tyson's next bout was against Sweden's undefeated Otto Wallin at the T-Mobile Arena in Las Vegas on September 14, 2019. Tyson dominated the action and won a WBC Mayan Belt commemorating the Mexican National Holiday. Then, plans were made for another Wilder matchup scheduled for February 2020. Tyson also began planning his autobiography and a documentary which will come out soon.

Tyson met Deontay Wilder for a rematch on February 22, 2020 at the MGM Grand in Las Vegas. Their second bout was quite different than the first. Tyson never gave Wilder much of a chance as he chased Deontay around the ring punishing him continuously. Wilder was knocked down in 3rd round and 5th round while he slipped down a couple of times from being pressured. Wilder's corner threw in the towel at the 7th round to hand over the WBC Championship title to Tyson. Tyson earned six different title belts in his pro career in addition to the lineal title all within thirty one bouts. Tyson is back on track for more wins and more titles! Tyson currently lives in Morecambe, England.

MY OBSERVATION

Wow! What a man! Tyson, a one-pound baby to a giant man of 6'9' and 260 pounds plus becoming the World Heavyweight Boxing Champion! You could make a movie about his life and Boxing career. He has not lost in his professional career and is still the last lineal Heavyweight Champion. He has had some personal issues, but he is back on track and is anxious to get back in the ring to defend his titles. Tyson is a very colorful man and Heavyweight Champion!

ANTHONY JOSHUA

B: Oct. 15, 1989
B: Hertfordshire, England
6'6" / 250 lbs.
Record: 22-1 21 KO's

Champion:
Apr. 29, 2017 - Jun.1, 2019
Dec. 7,2019 - Present

Anthony Joshua was born to Robert and Yeta Joshua of Nigeran descent, in their adopted country of England. Anthony spent much of his childhood in Nigeria until he was twelve years old, then moved back to Hertfordshire, England. Anthony was a naturally talented athlete who loved sports, including football and running track in school.

Anthony took up Boxing at age eighteen at the Finchley ABC Boxing Club in North London and became very good, very quickly. He won the Haringey Boxing Cup in 2009 and 2010, the ABA Championship in 2010, and was named Amateur Boxer of the Year in 2011. He also won the Gold medal in the Super-Heavyweight division in the Olympic Summer Games held in London, England in 2012 after four close bouts. His amateur career ended with a record of 40 wins and only four losses.

Anthony turned pro and took on Emanuele Leo of Italy in a six-rounder at the O2 Arena in London on October 5, 2013. It was an early night as Anthony barely broke a sweat and TKO'd Leo in the first round. Anthony then took on seven more opponents in Great Britain in the next year who all fell before the 3rd round by TKO or KO.

Anthony's next bout was two-time WBC International Champ, Denis Bakhtov of Russia, for that vacant WBC International title in London on October 11, 2014. Anthony stopped Bakhtov at the first minute in round two to secure his first title belt.

Nearly a year later, on September 12, 2015, Anthony faced Brit Gary Cornish for the vacant Commonwealth Title Belt, again at the O2 Arena in London. It was another easy win as Anthony TKO'd Cornish in the first round to take home his second Championship Belt.

Only seven months later, American Charles Martin appeared on the scene as the competitor who held the IBF Heavyweight Crown. Their meeting also took place at the O2 Arena on April 9, 2016. Martin only lasted halfway through the 2nd round before Anthony KO'd him and took his title home. This was Anthony's third title in just two and a half years.

Anthony took on two more Americans, Dominic Breazeale, and Eric Molina, who both fell by TKO in England before he faced his biggest challenge of his career, Wladimir Klitschko. Klitschko had been the lineal Champion for nearly six and a half years and seemed invincible. However, Anthony was ready on April 29, 2017, at Wembley Stadium in London. Both big men traded punches and knockdowns, but Anthony kept punching and punishing Klitschko until he moved to the ropes. Tonight, Klitschko couldn't take the punishment anymore as Joshua was awarded another TKO victory at the end of round eleven. Anthony had just added the vacant WBA Super Heavyweight and IBO titles to his collection.

Next on the list was Frenchman Carlos Takam, who went down in defeat via another TKO in the 10th round at the Principality Stadium in Wales on October 28, 2017. Joseph Parker of New Zealand tried his luck at the Venue six months later and is credited with being the only opponent to avoid Joshua's regular TKO and KO process. Parker survived, but lost a Unanimous

Decision to go home empty-handed. Next up, Russian Alexander Povetkin made his attempt on September 22, 2018, in Wembley Stadium, but also fell by TKO in the 7th round.

Underdog, Andy Ruiz Jr. was eventually given a shot after several other contenders couldn't come to an agreement. The contest took place in Madison Square Garden in New York on Saturday, June 1, 2019. It seemed to be another day at the office when Anthony dropped Ruiz in the third round. However, it appeared to wake Ruiz after he rose to drop Anthony twice in this same round. The back and forth continued, but after Anthony suffered two more knockdowns in the 7th round and after too much punishment, the referee stepped in to give Ruiz a TKO win over Anthony. Ruiz, the first Mexican American World Heavyweight Champion, walked away with the WBA Superheavyweight, IBF, WBO, and IBO Heavyweight titles. It was Anthony's only pro loss after he had won every bout in his career by TKO and KO, except just one Unanimous Decision.

Anthony and Ruiz Jr. had a highly anticipated rematch on December 7, 2019 in Saudia Arabia.

Former Champion Anthony

Joshua was far more careful and calculating this time. Ruiz was again the underdog, and began stalking Anthony in the rematch without delay. Anthony wisely used consistent jabs while constantly moving away from the dangerous Champion. Anthony also offered fewer right hands and hooks which caused him trouble in his only pro loss to Ruiz.

Ruiz only won two rounds in this last Championship match up of the decade, but landed some overhands that were just dangerously short. Anthony won the 12 round Unanimous Decision to regain his Championship titles and once again become Boxing royalty.

MY OBSERVATION

Anthony Joshua has the appearance of a Champion with his good looks and athletic physique. Before Andy Ruiz Jr, Anthony put down every opponent in his professional career except one Unanimous Decision, which included the invincible Wladimir Klitschko. Anthony had a perfect strategy in the first Andy Ruiz Jr. contest until he tried to slug with a "slugger". I believe that Anthony underestimated Ruiz Jr. in their first match, but was wise to stay away and not trade punches in their rematch on December 7, 2019.

ANDY RUIZ JR.

B: Sept. 11, 1989
6' 2" / 245 lbs.
Record: 33-1 22 KO's

Champion:
June 1, 2019 – Dec. 7, 2019

Andy Ponce Ruiz Jr. was born in Imperial, California, to parents who immigrated to the US from Mexicali, Mexico. His grandfather owned a Boxing gym in Mexicali and had several winning students himself. Andy's father got Junior into Boxing when he was just seven years old in nearby San Diego. As Andy trained and continued his amateur career, he worked with his father in construction.

As Andy trained with his father and developed for several years, he won two Mexican National Olympic Gold Medals, and a Ringside World Championship title. He also represented Mexico in the 2008 Olympics in Beijing. He finished his amateur career with an excellent record of 105 wins to only five losses.

Andy's first three pro bouts were in Mexico, two in China, and one in New Zealand. All other twenty-eight bouts took place in the US against names that were journeymen and champions of limited titles. He won his first nineteen fights in four years and mixed his wins with a combination of TKO, KO's, and Unanimous Decisions.

Andy flew to China to meet American Joe Hanks for his first title shot and the vacant WBO Intercontinental Heavyweight belt. The trip was worth it as Andy had very little trouble winning by KO over Hanks in the 4th round to return home the new WBO Champion.

Andy returned to the Far East just four months later to take on American Tor Hamer for the vacant NABF Heavyweight title. Andy took another easy win and the title as Hamer retired after the 3rd round giving Andy his second belt.

The new Champion of two belts cruised through eight more victories before meeting Joseph Parker of New Zealand at Vector Arena in Auckland for the WBO Heavyweight title. Andy was victorious again against

Parker then chalked up three more wins against two Americans and a German in California.

After Anthony Joshua had three unsuccessful agreements with others, Andy was awarded the chance to fight the WBA Super Heavyweight, IBF, WBO, and IBO Heavyweight title holder, Joshua. They met in Madison Square Garden on Saturday, June 1, 2019, for the fight of Andy's life. Andy was an unknown to many Boxing fans and was the underdog.

Joshua seemed to be ready to eliminate Andy in the third round after a knockdown, the first in his career. However, the knockdown just seemed to wake Andy. He got up and dropped Joshua twice in the very same round. Andy stalked while Joshua worked defense in rounds four, five, and six until Andy dropped Joshua twice more in the seventh round. This prompted the referee to step in and give the win to Andy by TKO. This was one of the biggest upsets in Heavyweight Boxing history as Andy Ruiz Jr. took the titles to become the first Mexican-American World Heavyweight Champion.

After Anthony Joshua lost, he focused on getting his titles back as he went home to London, England to regroup. Now Champion Andy Ruiz Jr., went home to Imperial California to his wife and five children with his Championship title belts in hand.

However, Anthony Joshua only let Andy have the title for six months.

MY OBSERVATION

Andy wanted to get back on the inside and slug in their December 2019 rematch, but Joshua wasn't having it. Joshua jabbed and moved for the entire bout to avoid Andy's exceptional hook punches and overhands.

Andy just couldn't catch or corner Joshua to retain the World Heavyweight Championship in their rematch. Their December 7, 2019 bout was the last Heavyweight Championship of the decade. However, Andy Ruiz Jr. became a Heavyweight Boxing star in 2019!

Andy Ruiz Jr. surprised the Boxing World on June 1, 2019. He hadn't fought the big names, which made it hard to predict his true abilities. Andy didn't have the athletic physique or the reach advantage, but he had a good defense and hard punches. He reminds me of David Tua and James Toney, who were shorter with less reach, so had to slip, bob, and weave before attacking. When Andy gets on the inside, he's a good finisher like Jack Dempsey, Joe Frazier or Mike Tyson. I thought that the referee stopped the June 1, bout a little too early for a Championship bout. The fight plan in the December rematch is what I expected from Anthony Joshua.

HEAVYWEIGHT BOXING QUIZ

1 - Who modernized Boxing in 1719 in London, England?

2- Who is the last Heavyweight Champion of the 2019?

3- Who was the first official gloved and lineal Heavyweight Champion?

4- Who is the only undefeated Heavyweight Champion?

5- Who lived to be the oldest Heavyweight Champion?

6- Who is the first modern Olympic Gold medalist to become Heavyweight Champion?

7- Who was the shortest man that became Heavyweight Champion?

8- Who had the longest reign as Heavyweight Champion?

9- Who were the first brothers that won the Heavyweight Championship?

10-Who was the youngest man to become the Heavyweight Champion?

11- Who was the last Bareknuckle Champion?

12- What are the current rules of Boxing called?

13- Who was known as the "Manassa Mauler"?

14- Who was the first southpaw Heavyweight Champion?

15- Who were the brothers to hold Heavyweight Championships simultaneously?

16- Who was the Champion that Jack Dempsey took the title from?

17- Who were the Champions that beat every opponent that they faced?

18- Who was the winningest Heavyweight that never became Champion?

19- Who became known as the "Cinderella Man"?

20- Who was the first man to regain the lineal Championship?

21- Who was the Champion that only weighed one pound at birth?

22- Who was the gloved Heavyweight Champion that had the shortest reign?

23- Who was the only man to survive 15 rounds with Rocky Marciano?

24- Who dethroned "Iron" Mike Tyson?

25- Who was the first African-American Heavyweight Champion?

26- Who was the Champion that had a son on a TV show in the 1960's?

27- Who was the tallest Heavyweight Champion?

28- Who was a Boxing Heavyweight Champion and a Wrestling Champion?

29- Who was Muhammad Ali's biggest nemesis?

30- Who is the richest Heavyweight Boxer?

31- Who are the two men that were crowned Champion without a fight?

32- Who was the "Cincinnati Cobra"?

33- Who was a lineal Light and lineal Heavyweight Champion?

34- Who were the Olympic Gold Medalists that became Heavyweight Champion?

35- Who are the five men that became two-time lineal Champions?

36- Who were the two Boxers involved in the first "Long Count"?

37- Who won the Heavyweight Championship via foul/disqualification?

38- Who was the oldest man to become the lineal Heavyweight Champion?

39- Who did Rocky Marciano take the title from?

40- Who was called "The Brown Bomber"?

41- Who was the first gloved Heavyweight Champion from England?

42- Who was responsible for the term "Phantom Punch"?

43- Who was the Heavyweight Champion called "The Bear"?

44- Who were the four Heavyweight Champions born in Brooklyn, New York?

45- Who became Heavyweight Champion by a six-man box-off to fill Muhammad Ali's vacant title?

46- Who are the two Heavyweight Champions that had their own singing group?

47- Who was the Champion that left Boxing for ten years before returning?

48- Who was the opponent that broke Muhammad Ali's jaw?

49- Who was the Heavyweight Champion that tried to surpass Rocky Marciano's record?

50- Who was the only Undefeated Light Heavyweight that beat an Undefeated Heavyweight Champion?

51- Who was the 46-0 underdog that beat the current Heavyweight Champion?

52- Who was the only three-time lineal Heavyweight Champion?

53- Who was the opponent that had part of his ear bitten off?

54- Who was the only man to TKO Evander Holyfield?

55- Who was the man that lost the title to George Foreman on his comeback?

56- Who was the first Middleweight Champ to beat the Heavyweight Champion?

57- Who was deemed the first American Bareknuckle Champion?

58- Who was the first Olympic Gold Medal Champion in 688BC?

59- Who devised the first set of Boxing rules?

60- Who was the first two-time Heavyweight Champion?

61- Who was the first Heavyweight to be inducted into the "Over 50 Knockout Club"?

62- Who is the Heavyweight Champion buried in Arlington National Cemetery?

63- Who built the first perimeter with a "Gate" to view their contest?

64- Who was the oldest Heavyweight to win the Championship?

65- Who is credited with inventing the "Dumbbell"?

66- Who was the Boxer that upset Champion, Floyd Patterson?

67- Who was also a Track and Field star in high school?

68- Who was the only Boxer to knockout Larry Holmes?

69- Who is credited with putting the color corner posts in the ring?

70- Who Called their overhand hook punch his "Susie Q"?

71- Who had a grandstand built for his bout?

72- Who was the first Boxer to beat Muhammad Ali?

73- Who was the first Middleweight, Light Heavyweight, and Heavyweight Champion?

74- Who had the shortest Championship reign in history?

75- Who was the only Boxer to beat Michael Spinks?

76- Who was awarded the first Championship Belt for the title?

77- Who held the Heavyweight Championship the longest?

78- Who was the first Champion to travel to other countries to defend his title?

79- Who was the only German Boxer to become the Heavyweight Champion?

80- Who earned 700 million dollars in his career and filed bankruptcy?

81- Who earned just $1.50 for his first bout?

82- Who was the Heavyweight Champion that loved baseball more than Boxing?

83- Who was the last Heavyweight Champion of the 19th Century?

84- Who was the 1st Olympic Gold Medalist to win the Heavyweight Championship?

85- Who was the only Mexican-American Heavyweight Champion?

86- Who won Championships for Canada and England?

87- Who has a bronze statue of him in Caesar's Palace?

88- Who decided to begin Boxing because of a Champion Boxer in the neighborhood?

89- Who was the Heavyweight Champion that was in the first televised Boxing match?

90- Who was the first non-American to win the Olympic Gold and Heavyweight title?

91- Who were the two Boxers that met in the "Rumble in the Jungle"?

92- Who was the tough street guy from Baltimore who became Champion?

93- Who was the only Swede to win the Heavyweight Championship?

94- Who was named the "Greatest Athlete of the 20th Century"?

95- Who has an asteroid named after them?

96- Who were the four Heavyweight Champions from Louisville KY?

97- Who did George Foreman recapture the Heavyweight Championship from?

98- Who was the first Light Heavyweight Champion to beat the Heavyweight Champ?

99- Who was the first Boxer to knock down Rocky Maricano?

100- Who was the only Italian Boxer to win the Heavyweight Championship?

101- Who was the only four-time Heavyweight Champ in history, (not lineal)?

Answers to quiz available at
www.terrymiddletons.com/boxquiz

KENTUCKIANA
BOXING TRAINERS

L ouisville, Kentucky has had four Heavyweight Boxing Champions dating back to Marvin Hart's title in 1905. Muhammad Ali won his first title in 1964, Jimmy Ellis in 1968, and Greg Page in 1984.

Incidentally, Louisville is the first and only other city in the world to have four Heavyweight Champions. Therefore, I thought it would only be appropriate to recognize some of the local trainers of the last 70 or so years here in my book. These coaches are primarily responsible for many young people becoming successful in Boxing and life. I have had the opportunity to connect with each one of them, beginning with the famed trainer Joe Martin.

Joe's Columbia Gym was on the lower floor of what became Spalding College in downtown Louisville, Kentucky. Joe is credited with introducing young Cassius Clay to Boxing. Mr. Martin was also responsible for a Boxing series called "Tomorrow's Champions" on WAVE-TV on Saturdays in the 1950's. This iconic trainer additionally hosted the Kentucky Golden Gloves tournaments at a local high school for years. I met with Joe several times as he helped me host Boxing and Kickboxing shows plus Karate tournaments. Joe also had other successful Boxers in his 1950's club including, Jimmy Ellis, and Billy Martin, and Fred Stoner.

Trainer, Bud Bruner was also a Boxing genius from Louisville who had several Boxing gyms beginning in the 1950's. Ultimately, future World Champion, Jimmy Ellis, became a student at Bud's gym. Bud was a meticulous and methodical trainer that seasoned Jimmy and prepared him for the World Championship belt. Jimmy then signed with promoter Don King and won a "Box Off" tournament to become World Heavyweight Champion in 1968 after Ali lost the title in 1967. Bruner had other successful Boxers including Rudell Stitch, who was ranked #2 in the world in the Welterweight division before a drowning accident in 1960. After Bud closed his last gym, he became a trainer at my gym in the 1980's training a few select Boxers.

Heavyweight Champion, Jimmy Ellis was an eager and gifted student of both, Joe Martin and Bud Bruner. Jimmy retired his career from the ring in 1975 and took on a few students of his own to train. One particular student was future World Cruiserweight Champion and U.S. Heavyweight Champion, James Pritchard. Ellis and Pritchard called our gym home while training and winning his titles until "Pritch" retired.

Billy Martin was included in the same Columbia Gym group with young Cassius Clay, Jimmy Ellis, and Fred Stoner in the 1950's. Billy and Fred were older and helped Joe Martin train the younger Boxers. Billy was a journeyman Boxer who stayed with Boxing and training his entire life. One day a co-worker asked Billy to teach his two sons how to box. Actually, both Greg and Dennis Page from Louisville, Kentucky were very athletic. Billy agreed and started the brothers off just across the Ohio river at a recreation center in downtown New Albany, Indiana. Greg followed Billy's close instructions and ultimately became the World Heavyweight Champion with a win over "Irish," Jerry Quarry in 1984. Billy was a great trainer and dedicated person at my gym for over 20 years.

Bud Schardein, Larry Alvey, and Tyrone Moore were among the stablemates of trainer Bud Bruner in the 1970's and early 1980's. Bud Schardein was a fierce competitor who also helped Bruner operate his gyms in Louisville's West End. After his competitive years, Bud helped train other Boxers at Bruner's gym and when Bruner moved over to my gym in the 1980's, so did Bud Schardein. In recent years, Bud has given unselfishly of his time and energy to local underprivileged kids in my gym. His passion was to help direct their lives in a positive way. Bud has a big heart and is a very dear friend who continues to support my gym to this day!

Larry Alvey also trained with Bud Schardein in the 1970's and early 1980's at Bruner's gym in Louisville. Larry was also a successful Boxer who became an accomplished trainer after retiring his career. Larry coached a very successful group of Boxers including one of my National Kickboxing Champions, Matt

Kitterman, who turned to Boxing. Larry coached Matt to a 20-0 Boxing record and a Silver Medal in the Boxing Olympics held in Russia in 2009. Matt also passed on his experience and coached some kids in his home town of Corydon, Indiana. Larry Alvey was a great friend and a great coach who gave many years to help others.

Louisvillians, Sammy Floyd and Tyrone Moore, were journeymen Middleweight Boxers who became Boxing referees and trainers after retiring from their career. They trained with some students at my gym over the years. Two great guys that very knowledgeable about the art and science of Boxing!

Doug Myers, James Doolin, Kelley Mays, William Jarvis, and James Roberts were also local Boxing trainers working out of gyms in Louisville, Kentucky. They all, except Roberts, worked out of my gym at one time or another.

Like the others, I was also a Louisvillian until my family moved just across the river to Indiana when I was 13 years old. I mentioned earlier that my Grandfather and Father boxed in the service, so I thought I would like to learn about Boxing in 1963. However, five years later, in 1968, I also found Karate classes to be exciting. I joined the first Martial Arts studio that opened in this area in Jeffersonville, Indiana. I practically lived at the school, so one day, the owner asked me to help out as an assistant instructor in 1969. After teaching there for three years, I started my own Martial Arts school in 1972. Since I had been exposed to Boxing, I added it to my program. Actually, at that time, people who trained in Karate and Boxing didn't believe the other Art was as effective and didn't want to train together. However, I saw the benefit of having them learn from each other and brought many of them together here in Kentuckiana.

Today, we still offer several other Arts at our operation. We are very proud of our very program that includes our successful 4th floor Boxing gym, now open for a half-century!

This information was gathered by the aforementioned references, my first-hand knowledge, family members, and stablemates of Trainers and Boxers.

The Four Heavyweight Champions From Louisville Kentucky

- **Marvin Hart**
- **Muhammad Ali**
- **Jimmy Ellis**
- **Greg Page**

Image by Boxer & Trainer Joel Cox

RICHEST BOXERS

Floyd Mayweather	$400,000,000
George Foreman	$250,000,000
Oscar DeLaHoya	$200,000,000
Manny Pacquiao	$190,000,000
Lennox Lewis	$140,000,000
Sugar Ray Leonard	$120,000,000
Vitali Klitschko	$65,000,000
Muhammad Ali	$50,000,000
Marvin Hagler	$45,000,000
Roy Jones	$45,000,000
Bernard Hopkins	$40,000,000
Ricky Hatton	$40,000,000
Naseem Hamed	$33,000,000
Felix Trinidad	$30,000,000
Anthony Mundine	$30,000,000
Amir Khan	$30,000,000
Joe Calzaghe	$21,000,000
Carl Froch	$20,000,000
Juan Manuel Marquez	$20,000,000
Larry Holmes	$18,000,000

AUTHOR'S NOTE

I have watched Boxing Matches both on film and personally back to the days of many World Heavyweight Champions. There are some consistencies that I would like to point out.

The challenger of a title bout seems to be more motivated for the victory as his long-time goal seems to be within reach. The challenger also has had his eye on the Champion assessing his strengths and weaknesses. Many times, this is the key to defeating the Champion.

After some time, the Champion seems mentally content and has a sense of accomplishment. His major goal has been achieved and often doesn't focus as before. In addition to a Champion's mental state, there is simply the factor of age. If the Champion has had a long reign, his physical abilities will naturally decline.

Many times, after a Champion loses his title, he regroups and tries to regain his crown. He strongly believes that he can, but the odds are greatly against him, as history proves. Most former Champions are not successful in comebacks, but can earn large needed purses, however, at the risk of serious physical harm.

They are also very likely to tarnish their excellent record and image that they worked so hard to earn in their earlier career.

Note how many former Champions try a comeback and do not succeed!

Terry Middleton

Terry Middleton's
Karate, Boxing, & Kickboxing School
Established 1972
For more info visit www.terrymiddletons.com

Printed in the United States
by Baker & Taylor Publisher Services